Praise for SCARRED FAITH

"Josh Ross does not write about suffering as an expert, a theologian, or a pastor—though, in some sense, he is all three. *Scarred Faith* is an honest and raw description of life with God in the dark moments of pain and loss. This is not a book for those who want a Disney Jesus. This is a book for the rest of us, who, day by day, are learning to allow God to draw close to us in the midst of—not in spite of—our doubts, questions, and anxiety. Josh is a witness to the truth that God allows us to take on the strength of that which we overcome. So, read. And be strong in God."

—Josh Graves, author of *Heaven on Earth* and
The Feast: Realizing the Good Life

"If you prefer a domesticated and sanitized faith, DON'T READ THIS BOOK! Josh asks hard questions, deep questions, the kind that people only ask who care as deeply as they hurt. But if you have been wounded and if the pain of the world breaks your heart, READ THIS BOOK! You will find hope and courage, not to remove your scars, but to redeem them."

—Rick Atchley, senior minister of The Hills Church in
Fort Worth, Texas

"This book clung to me for days after I read the first draft. Here Josh Ross walks us into places where God makes no sense to us—and where, on the face of things, He appears to be anything but a good God. The writing style is fresh and creative, but the real genius lies in the way Josh draws the reader up close to raw and inexplicable pain and loss—yet also reveals a way to embrace our pain, rather than to run from it. Ross calls us to be 'scarred with God' because God is willing to redirect overwhelming grief into enormous positive energy. A really helpful read for those of us who suffer—and for those who care."

—Lynn Anderson, Hope Network Ministries

"Reading *Scarred Faith* reminds us that even when death and painful suffering knock us off the busy sidewalk of life into a dark alley of hopelessness, even when we stop believing that a doorway of beauty will open up for us, God arrives. Josh writes beautifully, and with brutal honesty, about the loss of his sister Jenny and brings us closer to the understanding that God dwells in the allies of grief and loss, and it is here that we can find a peace beyond all understanding. This book will challenge you to really dig deep and ask yourself: what is it again that I *truly* believe?"

—Pam Cope, Touch A Life Foundation

"*Scarred Faith* is a must read for anyone who wants to go deep with God. Josh Ross has captured the true essence of what it means to walk a life with Christ. Sometimes we celebrate answered prayers and sometimes we don't understand, but in the end Jesus wins. Adventure, heartache, childhood to adulthood, *Scarred Faith* covers the meaning of growing closer to Christ through everything that we endure and enjoy in life. You will not be able to put this book down."

—Tommy Maddox, Super Bowl champion and former NFL quarterback

"If faith always works the way it should for you, if your prayers are always answered, if you're always living in the delight of a spiritual summer, this book may just puzzle you. But if you have battled doubt, if you have agonized over God's apparent silence, if you've felt gusts of winter chilling your spiritual journey—well, this is your book. Ross writes with raw honesty about life's disappointments but also with bold hope about God's future. I look forward to putting it in the hands of many people who are struggling to believe among life's disappointments."

—Mike Cope, director of Ministry Outreach, Pepperdine University, and author of *Megan's Secrets: What My Mentally Disabled Daughter Taught Me About Life*

"Every few years, a book comes along that inspires you to re-examine your life and your purpose according to what Christ truly has asked us to do as believers. *Scarred Faith* is such a book. Josh Ross writes with beautiful honesty and even humor as he fearlessly dives into a world marred by the ugliness of sin, suffering, grief, and tragedy. Joshua seeks not to answer the question 'Why does God allow bad things to happen to good people?' But he instead shows us—from first-hand experience—God's intention that good people use the bad things that have happened to redeem the world around them with the love of Christ. If you were only to read a few books this year besides the Bible, *Scarred Faith* should be one of them."

—Dudley Rutherford, author of *God Has an App for That!: Discover God's Solutions for the Major Issues of Life*

"Although Josh Ross is not a native Memphian, his book *Scarred Faith* demonstrates that he reflects some of the most precious values for which our city is known, namely, resilience and faith in God. He has embraced ministry in our city with the type of zeal and deep affection that one would possibly only expect from those with longstanding familial and social connections here. It just shows that Josh Ross is truly one of us—by geography and by spirit."

—A C Wharton, Jr., mayor of Memphis, Tennessee

"Sometimes wisdom comes from unexpected places. Josh Ross has written a book that speaks to the human experience and provides a compassionate answer for all of those who have lost a loved one and, with it, their faith. Weaving together the story of losing his beloved sister with lessons of how that loss challenged his faith as an ordained Christian minister, Ross bravely shares with us his own anger and doubt caused by the failure of his prayers and petitions to save his sister. He then leads us to a deeper exploration of the true Christian journey by recognizing that our emotional scars carry with them the opportunity for grace. Ross was inspired to move his young family to one of the poorest neighborhoods in Memphis, Tennessee, in order to heal himself and to live out the true social gospel of Jesus of Nazareth. As a mother who lost her own son just four years ago, *Scarred Faith* assures me that my pain can be used to humbly serve others and, in the process, heal myself. It is a book of simplicity, subtlety, and beauty that needs to be shared with the world."

—Gayle S. Rose, chief executive officer
of Electronic Vaulting Services

SCARRED FAITH

This is a story about how

Honesty

Grief

A Cursing Toddler

Risk-Taking

AIDS

Hope

Brokenness

Doubts

and Memphis

Ignited Adventurous Faith

JOSH ROSS

HOWARD BOOKS
A DIVISION OF SIMON & SCHUSTER, INC.

New York   Nashville   London   Toronto   Sydney   New Delhi

Howard Books
A Division of Simon & Schuster, Inc.
1230 Avenue of the Americas
New York, NY 10020

First Howard Books trade paperback edition May 2013

HOWARD and colophon are trademarks of Simon & Schuster, Inc.

For information about special discounts for bulk purchases,
please contact Simon & Schuster Special Sales at 1-866-506-1949
or business@simonandschuster.com.

The Simon & Schuster Speakers Bureau can bring authors to your live event. For more information or to book an event, contact the Simon & Schuster Speakers Bureau at 1-866-248-3049 or visit our website at www.simonspeakers.com.

Designed by Jill Putorti

Manufactured in the United States of America

10   9   8   7   6   5   4   3   2   1

Library of Congress Cataloging-in-Publication Data

Ross, Josh.
   Scarred faith : this is a story about how honesty, grief, a cursing toddler, risk-taking, AIDS, hope, brokenness, doubts, and Memphis ignited adventurous faith / Josh Ross.
       p. cm.
   1. Suffering—Religious aspects—Christianity. I. Title.
   BV4909.R67 2012
   248.8'6—dc23
           2012027633
ISBN 978-1-4516-8821-4
ISBN 978-1-4516-8822-1 (ebook)

To Jenny:

*Much of what I have learned about grief
came through your death.*

I would trade this book for your life any day of the week.

Your faith lives on.

You continue to inspire me.

CONTENTS

FOREWORD

I am sitting on the terrace of my home in Dorset, Vermont. The newly risen sun is gathering strength. It pierces the leafy canopy above my head and marbles my lawn with dappling light. In the space between my favorite maples a cloud passes, a puffy interloper in an otherwise pristine sky. My children are safe in their beds, but soon they will wake and insist we go swimming at a nearby pond. It is an idyllic tableau.

Why, when I am surrounded by so much untarnished beauty, have I decided to read a book with the portentous title *Scarred Faith*? Why have I read it nearly twice in two days?

The answer is I like writers who belly up to the bar and order the truth. I particularly admire writers of faith who refuse to practice the politics of evasion and instead choose to face squarely the cruel calculus of human suffering. This might sound gloomy if not draconian, but my age, the scriptures, my own experiences of loss and grief, and what I have witnessed of other people's anguish won't allow me to equivocate. Denial is no match for the truth. We suffer. There is no other way to be in the world.

For me the greatest source of consolation in times of anguish has come from those souls who bravely open their hearts and relay their own journey from darkness to light, from despair to resurrection. Saints who have suffered well—like Job, King David, Desmond Tutu, Mother Teresa, or Elie Wiesel—come alongside us and, with words born from brokenness, share how the mysterious thread of grace that weaves through all things eventually revealed itself to them.

Josh Ross is this kind of author. In sharing his own story of loss and grief he helps us to make sense of our own.

Christianity, Josh reminds us, is unique among the religions of the world in its assertion that God's answer to those who mourn is neither a sermon nor an academic treatise but a person, namely Jesus. We are sustained by the belief that God has punched a hole in the roof of our world and inserted himself into the human drama, opting to suffer as we suffer. In our pain we demand answers, and Heaven gently replies, "Jesus. Emmanuel. God with us." These are the facts. Everything else is editorial.

Be forewarned. Joshua's story is more than just a well-told personal narrative. The life decisions he made in the wake of his tragic experience reveal that suffering is not something to be endured as much as stewarded. Joshua compassionately but firmly challenges us to move beyond asking "Why am I suffering?" and live into the question "What does my pain make possible?"

This wise and instructive book written by someone who has walked through the debris field of a terrible loss and *lived* the answer to this all-important question will deeply move you.

Countless works have been written on the theme of loss and redemption, and more will be written in the future, but this one stands out on the shelf. *Scarred Faith* has enriched my soul. Anyone with eyes to see and ears to hear will find it a pearl bought and shared at great price.

Ian Morgan Cron
author of *Jesus, My Father, the CIA, and Me: A Memoir of Sorts*
Dorset, Vermont

SCARRED FAITH

> I am drawn to Jesus, irresistibly, because he positioned himself as the dividing point of life—my life. . . . Sometimes I accept Jesus' audacious claim without question. Sometimes, I confess, I wonder what difference it should make to my life that a man lived two thousand years ago in a place called Galilee. Can I resolve this inner tension between doubter and lover?
>
> —PHILIP YANCEY[1]

Deep faith is scarred faith.

Faith can be stirred within the walls of church buildings, but faith is formed and nourished in the waiting rooms of hospitals, helplessly witnessing a thirty-one-year-old sister suffer, holding kids affected by the AIDS epidemic, and being stretched outside of our own social makeup.

It's a good thing to be able to memorize the names of the sixty-six books of the Bible by the age of five, but not if you've never had a meal with someone from another race by the age of sixteen. Not if you've never shaken a hand in a soup kitchen. Not if you don't know the names of your neighbors.

A guy walked into my office a while back. I was fairly new to Memphis at the time, but he had literally spent years of his life on its streets. His worn-down body slumped in my recliner, and I could sense his heavy burden. He looked depressed, physically and mentally drained. He had recently entered into an AA program, and one of the Twelve Steps encourages the confession of sins. I'm not a priest. A black suit with a white collar is quite different from my everyday wardrobe, which consists of blue jeans with a golf shirt, shirttail hanging out. We didn't know each other very well, but he felt like I was a safe place for him to unload the secrets of his life. He took a deep breath and then began confessing.

"Josh, let me begin at the age of fourteen when I murdered someone for the first time."

Okay, in my decade of full-time ministry I've heard all kinds of confessions. I've heard about adultery, cheating on taxes, pornography, racism, masturbation, cheering for the Yankees, and teenagers seeking advice because they got a tattoo without their parents' consent. This was the first time I felt uneasy about a confession. Maybe it's because he said "for the *first* time," meaning there were more murder confessions coming. Maybe it's because he was sitting between me and the door, and my mind immediately began going through scenarios of what I'd do if he lifted his street-smart body from my recliner and approached me with both hands stretched out for a stranglehold. I calmed myself. I had seen three seasons of *24*, and when in difficult situations like this, who wouldn't ask, "What would Jack Bauer do?"

For the next forty-five minutes I heard about thirty years of complete brokenness and pain. He laid it all out in front of me, year after year of betrayal and utter darkness. For a moment I wanted to hit Pause on our conversation in order to call my mom and dad to thank them for a wonderful childhood. I thought I had it rough because my parents refused to buy us automotive vehicles when we turned sixteen. My new friend had only been a Christ follower for a couple of years, but he felt lost, unforgiven, and guilty. He defined the first thirty years of his life as a complete failure. And that's when I interrupted, feeling the need to speak Christ into this situation.

"Listen here. Do you believe that God has the power to redeem you? Do you believe that God can rewrite the next thirty years of your life? Do you believe that he has the power to usher you into a better story—a story that will be so beautiful, so glorious, so redeeming that your life will bear witness to the power of the resurrection of Jesus? You are a man with physical and emotional scars. Do you believe that God can redeem your scars?"

He lifted his head. The brokenness was still evident, but there was a look of hope that asked, "Is there really a God who can redeem these scars?"

Isn't that the good news of the Jesus story? Faith isn't about forgetting the past, but redeeming the past. It's the story of a God who is able to recreate from life's scars.

Deep faith is scarred faith.

Faith isn't something that is downloaded into a brain like antivirus software onto a desktop. It is about lived experiences. Faith doesn't run deep because one is stuffed with right answers. It is cultivated by asking the right questions. Faith is about journey, experience, movement, and process. It is about adventure. And one thing we know about adventure is that there are moments of pain, regret, wounds, suspense, and questioning.

And so we receive this two-word invitation from Jesus: "Follow me." We would much rather focus on words like "Accept me" and "Believe in me," because these phrases tend to be more about the mind and what we believe in our hearts. But "Follow me" is an invitation into life. It's not about Jesus getting into our hearts so much as it is about us getting into Jesus. It is physical as much as it is mental.

To respond to these two words might just wreck your life as you know it. Or so it has mine.

■   ■   ■

I did something when my oldest son was only three weeks old that most first-time dads don't do: I went skydiving. I can still remember driving south of Houston on I-45 drinking 5-hour ENERGY shots with my friends, as if we really needed an energy boost considering we were within a few hours of free-falling from thirteen thousand feet at a speed of 120 miles per hour.

The anxiety was building as we got dressed in our blue jumpsuits. A thirty-minute instruction video provided comic relief as we were forced to practice our free-falling skills while lying facedown on the carpet. It was a moment for grown men to become like fifteen-year-old boys in a locker room.

My breathing was back to normal until one of our instructors said, "Hey, we're minutes away from boarding the plane. I'll be right back. I'm going to see if I can find a parachute that works." Needless to say, we entered into freak-out mode again.

Halfway up in the plane, the professional I was jumping with leaned over my shoulder, and over the loud engine he screamed, "When you go home, go to YouTube and type in 'Wildest Weddings,' and you can watch my wedding ceremony."

So, I did it.

Check this out: this guy and his bride-to-be were on an airplane. He was in a tux; she was dressed in pants with a white top. The minister sat on the plane in front of them and had them recite their vows.

"Do you take this woman to be your wife?"

"I do."

Then, looking at the bride: "Do you take this man to be your husband?"

"Yes, but, if you want me, you have to come and get me." She turned toward the door of the plane and jumped out. The groom didn't hesitate. He jumped out after her.

The four-team video crew was filming a wedding taking place between fifteen thousand and five thousand feet in the air. Dropping at a rate of five seconds per one thousand feet doesn't give you much time to exchange rings and kisses, but they did it. Think how crazy this is: it's one thing for a woman to put a guy's ring on his finger while free-falling at ridiculous speeds because it only costs a couple hundred bucks, but it's another thing to exchange a ring that has a fat rock on it.

Fortunately, they were able to pull their parachutes, and when they hit the ground—or, better said, when they *landed* on the ground—a minister ran over to the landing spot to pronounce them husband and wife.

How's that for adventure?

We love adventures because of the thrill and sheer magnitude of suspense. It usually involves close friends or relatives, because adventures aren't nearly as fun if you're alone. Adventures provide memories that will last a lifetime. In fact, nonadventurous people are usually lousy communicators, because their Rolodex of life is often void of authentic experiences.

But most of us have a love/hate relationship with adventures.

Adventures involve sacrifice, time, and commitment. Whether it's the churning stomach of a free fall or the soreness of pounding-the-concrete training for a marathon, adventures cost something.

It's interesting, as one friend says, that Jesus spent most of his time trying to get people to take seriously the life that is lived outside of the Temple, yet we have spent nearly two thousand years trying to get life back into a Temple. It's much easier to have a Bring a Friend Day at church than it is to have a Be the Church Day. One involves inviting friends to come inside of a church so that the worship minister and teaching pastor can lead them to Jesus. The other involves people taking their own lives into the streets and neighborhoods to become living sacrifices or, as many say now, to become the hands and feet of Jesus.

When faith fails to acknowledge the power of adventure, it soon becomes wrapped in discrete forms of legalism that strangle the joy of following Jesus in the present world.

Faith without adventure is reduced to crossing our fingers and hoping that we get into heaven in the end instead of answering the radical call of Jesus to experience the abundant life that he has to offer in the here and now.

To strip adventure and risk taking from faith and spirituality causes immense oppression, injustice, and brokenness throughout our world, because people no longer hear the voice of Jesus calling them into the places soaked with his breath, sweat, and tears. And if they *do* hear his voice, they are more prone to offer up a quick prayer or write a check than to restore dignity to people through handshakes, hugs, or any kind of actual touch.

"Follow me" is an invitation into the abundant life. In fact, however you choose to interpret "abundant life" will determine how you choose to live this life. If "abundant life" only means being with Jesus after you die, then you will most likely live as a person who will do little to advance the kingdom of God on this earth. But if you believe that the "abundant life" begins on earth, then you will enter into the joy of following the one who came claiming to be the Way, the Truth, and the Life, *right now.*

Adventures do something to us. They wake us up. They give us life.

But they also leave us with scars: permanent tattoos

bearing witness to the fact that we have lived life. Scars have stories, and they force us to ask questions:

- How did it get there?
- What caused it?
- Why did it happen?
- How did you survive?
- Who helped you?
- What was therapy like?
- How has it changed you?
- Where is God when it hurts?

No one solicits scars. We don't ask for them. We don't sign up for them. We don't endorse them. They just happen. The most painful scars might not be physical; they might be social, emotional, or personal.

Choosing to answer the invitation to follow Jesus will leave us with scar-worn bodies, or so this book will suggest. I'm inviting you on a journey with me. It begins autobiographically, but I think you'll quickly find that my story is one among many. In fact, we're all wrapped up in this greater narrative of a world that is groaning for redemption.

PART 1

WHEN SCARS RUN DEEP

One writer described Pope John Paul II's journey like this: "Ripped out of the soil of his background, his life could no longer be what it used to be. He now began a journey to deeper communion with God. But it didn't come without tears, and it didn't come without what seems to have been a certain existential horror." Suffering can do that to us. We're jolted, kicked, prodded, and shoved into new realities we never would have brought about on our own. We're forced to imagine a new future because the one we were planning on is gone.

—ROB BELL[1]

1

DOES GOD MAKE WRONG TURNS?

Will my eyes adjust to this darkness? Will I find you in the dark—not in the streaks of light which remain, but in the darkness? Has anyone ever found you there? Did they love what they saw? Did they see love? And are there songs for singing when the light has gone dim? The songs I learned were all of praise and thanksgiving and repentance. Or in the dark, is it best to wait in silence?

—NICHOLAS WOLTERSTORFF [1]

Life with Jesus is full of twists and turns. Some roads make sense. Some don't.

My close friend, Josh Graves, and I were both speaking at an event in Tulsa, Oklahoma. As we've done on a few occasions when we're at the same event, we shared a hotel room and a rental car. We woke up opening morning of the conference, got in the car to drive to the Tulsa Fairgrounds, and then realized that we didn't know how to get there. Two things would have saved us: 1) if one of us had

had a smartphone, but neither of us had upgraded, and 2) if Kara had been with us, Josh's wife, because she's like Sacagawea—she has a knack for directions. But we were without both.

Neither of us were Boy Scouts, but we were confident that we could find our way. It was about 8:20. Josh was to speak at 9:00. We were supposedly only ten minutes away. And the good news was we had a map.

Fifteen minutes and a few wrong turns later, we were reminiscent of a married couple in need of counseling.

He's yelling at me, "Do you not know how to read a map?"

I'm yelling back, "Do you not know how to listen to the person reading the map?"

He continues, "No, I'm not going to make an illegal U-turn!"

I'm responding, "Do you know what Terry Rush [the director of the event] will do to you if you're late? Make the U-turn!"

Then we did the thing that breaks Man Law 101: we pulled into a gas station to ask for directions. I walked in, and there were two men behind the counter standing shoulder to shoulder. I said, "Will one of you tell me how to get to the fairgrounds?" They both turned and pointed—in opposite directions.

They looked at each other and began arguing. I was about to speak to a group of people about imitating the character of Jesus, yet at that moment I was close to ruining my witness with a barrage of dirty words and obscenities.

I looked at Josh through the glass door, shrugging my shoulders in disbelief at what was happening. His mouth wasn't moving, but his nonverbals were a perfect depiction of a cross between nervousness, anger, and frustration.

In the end, despite a few wrong turns, we got directions and made it on time.

We live in a fast-paced world. It's a world in which we need things to run smoothly, because we don't do well with interruptions and unplanned events. No one plans for flat tires, stitches, or sinus infections.

So, when wrong turns happen in life, they can throw us a curve. They can disrupt our rhythm.

I hate wrong turns, because they take you off course. You're left with either finding new routes or making crazy U-turns. They test your patience and your integrity.

We all have stories of making wrong turns in this life. There are turns that have led us into sexual addictions, deep depressions, financial strains, and feelings of extreme loneliness. Wrong turns result in stiff-arming God and neglecting our neighbors.

However, on this journey of faith, do you ever feel like God has made a wrong turn in your life?

We have this story of the triumphal entry in Luke 19. Jesus rode into Jerusalem *on a colt.* Count on Jesus to choose a colt over a stallion or a first-century limo.

But the camera shifts to the crowd, because they weren't just there to witness this event; they were there with expectations of this event. They expected Jesus to ride into Jerusalem and to make the turns that would lead him to Herod's primary palace so that he could unseat the godless rulers to set up this thing he'd been talking about for a few years called the Kingdom of God. They expected Jesus to turn to the Temple so that he could establish a religion that would make things right.

In fact, Mark tells us that people were *following* Jesus, but he also says that people were *ahead* of Jesus.[2]

Why were the crowds walking ahead of him? It's because they thought they knew exactly where he was going.

They were shouting, "Hosanna!"—a song of salvation. A song sung with expectation.

The message of deliverance that religious leaders had been proclaiming for centuries was happening right before their eyes. It was a "Hosanna!" that was loaded with all kinds of agendas and expectations.

They expected Jesus to make things right, to conquer the powers of the world. But Jesus made a different turn. He turned to the cross.

It was as if Jesus had made a wrong turn.

■   ■   ■

I'm the middle child in my family—two years apart from both Jonathan, who is the youngest and most inquisitive, and Jenny, who has always been your quintessential protective oldest child. I remember a time when Jenny was babysitting us. She was thirteen, and she heard the sound of a train outside and immediately forced us into a hallway, where we sat under a mattress because she had seen a television show discussing tornadoes as sounding like trains. The only problem was that it was a clear, sunny day outside.

We grew up in a close family. To this day, I've never been on a plane with either one of my parents. We always took vacations in the light-blue Astro van. It was back in the late 1980s, when the Astro van was kind of cool. It officially qualified a mother of three as a soccer mom. From East Texas, we took long trips to Nashville, Yellowstone National Park, and Los Angeles. Occasionally, on our road trips, we would take hour-long detours to take pictures at historical markers like Billy the Kid's grave. Yes, we were *that* family.

This fullness of relationship was not something easily come by, though. My dad was a man who battled with depression, low self-esteem, and a childhood with an alcoholic father that left him scarred. However, he discovered that the heart of God was worth pursuing and that the resurrection of Jesus can raise people from the ashes, even before we die. He was committed to providing a childhood for all three of us that was unlike his own. He cultivated environments for us to discover the value of deep friendships and a close-knit family. The dinner table became a place to nurture a family more than it nurtured our bodies (and in no way is that a knock on my mom's cooking). Because of this, my siblings became two of my closest friends.

My dad, mom, Jonathan, and I received a text from Jenny on February 3, 2010, that her fever had spiked to 105. It wasn't too uncommon for a Ross. We don't get sick much, but when we run a fever, we go all out. My concern for Jenny on that day was that she had been sick for over five days. Immediately, I fell on my knees in my office and prayed for God's hand of mercy to touch Jenny's body. I received a text within the hour that her fever had broken. We thought this was good news.

The next morning I received a phone call from my mom that Jenny was in the ICU. She had gone to a medical clinic early in the morning, and after checking her blood pressure, they told her to go to the ER immediately. A specific strand of strep throat, Group A Strep, had forced the infection into her blood stream, and by the time she reached the ER her body was in a full-blown battle with septic shock.

I drove to Little Rock the next morning to catch a

flight on Southwest Airlines. Memphis is the largest city in Tennessee, yet we don't have Southwest. Every time I fly out of this city on my own dime my retirement is pushed back two years. The drive to Little Rock was surreal. A few hours later I was on a plane to the Dallas/Fort Worth area where I was expecting to walk into a hospital, see my sister recovering, and be back in Memphis the next night just in time to preach at Sycamore View the following morning. Call me naïve if you'd like, but I thought that if you didn't die from a car wreck, inexplicable tragedy, cancer, or a heart attack, scientific research and medical advancements would cure whatever ailed you.

I arrived as anesthetics were putting Jenny into a deep sleep. My mom, leaning over her sick body, said, "Jenny, Josh is here. Can you see him?" She managed to open both eyes and proceeded to nod her head yes. A few hours later the doctor met with my family in the hallway and spoke the words: "There's a fifty/fifty chance. She's the sickest person in any ICU in the DFW area."

Our world was suddenly crumbling. It seemed like God had made a wrong turn.

Maybe you were raised to believe that you could never question God's activity in the world or doubt his existence or he might just zap you with a lightning bolt. Maybe you think that the barrage of questions God deals Job toward the end of that bizarre book trumps every other moment of questioning and feeling of anger found in Scripture. In a context influenced so heavily by the Age of Enlightenment, which emphasized knowledge and intellect, the desperate need to believe with absolute assurance has suffocated the potential gift of asking hard questions.

You can keep your children from asking questions about life or even about God—until they get to college.

Are we allowed to say things like "God, this doesn't make any sense. Where are you?"

More important, does God honor seasons of doubt? Does God honor the questions we might have that come from moments of physical, social, or emotional pain?

Does James 1:6–8 become the ultimate trump card in this conversation? "But when you ask, you must believe and not doubt, because the one who doubts is like a wave of the sea, blown and tossed by the wind. Those who doubt should not think they will receive anything from the Lord; they are double-minded and unstable in all they do."

What about Matthew 28:17? Prior to the Great Commission, which is quoted in every Christian church, we are told that "they worshiped him; but some doubted." And Jesus still proceeds to give the Great Commission to the entire crowd. In other words, he doesn't separate the doubters from the worshippers. The worshippers include those who doubted. Jesus even commissions the doubters.

This adventure with Jesus demands honesty, and I

think God honors that. God is big enough and even willing enough to handle our questions, no matter how big they are.

February of 2010 left me scarred. The scars would force me to ask questions. And I leaned into the sovereignty and grace of God, believing that Jesus would be able to carry me through a season of uncertainty. After all, the same one who spoke the words "Follow me" also said, "I am with you always." I needed these words to be true.

2

THE FEBRUARY FROM HELL

All those years I fell for the great palace lie that grief should be gotten over as quickly as possible and as privately. But what I've discovered since is that the lifelong fear of grief keeps us in a barren, isolated place and that only grieving can heal grief; the passage of time will lessen the acuteness, but time alone, without the direct experience of grief, will not heal it.

—ANNE LAMOTT[1]

When I was a freshman in high school, I asked a girl if she wanted to go to the movies with me. Like it is for most freshmen, a date to the movies meant that Mom has to drop off a minivan full of ninth graders who are embarrassed to ride in a minivan. I don't even remember what movie we saw, but I remember that this girl had been on my radar and I was just thrilled to be at a movie with her. I wasted no time putting my arm around her, and before the movie was over, we had enjoyed the thrill of making out in a movie theater. (Give me some grace. I was in ninth grade.)

Later that night I called the girl to chat—this was before Facebook and text messaging—and a guy answered the phone—and let's just say he wasn't very happy. Little did I know that I was kissing a girl who was dating a senior from another school. This guy proceeded to tell me that if I ever called her again he was going to get his boys, come to my house, and kill me—literally. I heard someone pick up a phone on the other side of my house. It was my protective older sister, Jenny. She yelled, "Listen here, you little bastard! If you ever call over here again threatening my brother, I'm going to jump through this phone and kick your little ass!" He hung up. These were probably two of the five curse words Jenny said her entire life. A moment later, she rounded the corner with her fists in the air like she had come to save the day. Half of me wanted to jump up and congratulate her for her bravery. The other half of me felt deflated, because what would my friends say when they found out my sister was fighting my battles for me?

There are so many reasons why it was hard to walk into Jenny's ICU room. I arrived on Friday, February 5, at about 2:30 p.m. Even though I knew the seriousness of the sickness, I had no clue what I was walking into. Watching my thirty-one-year-old sister lying in a hospital bed was one of the most helpless feelings I have ever experienced in my life. I wanted to pull the tubes out and take her to a Mexi-

can food joint where we could indulge in table-side gua-
camole and beef enchiladas. I wanted to pack up our bags
and go to her favorite vacation place in the world—San
Antonio—where we could eat homemade tortillas from
Mi Tierra. But I couldn't. All I could do was stand there by
her bed praying and crying.

A prayer movement of over ten thousand people began,
as people prayed around the clock for Jenny's healing. We
knocked down the doors of heaven for God to speak the
word over her sick body. I leaned hard into Isaiah 55:11:
"So is my word that goes out from my mouth:/It will not
return to me empty,/but will accomplish what I desire/and
achieve the purpose of which I sent it." We had faith that
God's healing word performs. We clung to any hope we
could find. After all, healing just seemed right.

Why should a husband lose his wife?

Why should my nine-year-old niece live the rest of her
life without her mom?

Jenny and Malaya had a special bond from birth. Jenny was
married at nineteen. As a young teenager, she didn't just
fantasize about her wedding day; she dreamed of having a
quiver full of children. In a culture where many people are
fine fielding a tennis team (a one-person show or possibly
a pair), Jenny wanted a dozen.

At the age of twenty-one, barely over a year into their

marriage, she discovered she was pregnant. David nearly fainted, because they weren't even trying to have a child. Malaya was the miracle baby, and she stole the hearts of everyone in our family.

After Malaya was born, it wasn't long before Jenny was ready for Bizaillion number two. (Yes, she married a man with the last name Bizaillion. Don't think our family didn't chuckle about this for weeks after we found out.) However, this time wouldn't be so easy. Little did she know that she was entering into a nearly decade-long battle with infertility. They tried everything. Years of tests, procedures, needles, pills, doctor visits, and pregnancy tests, and she kept getting the same answer—barrenness. David and Jenny were at the point of wishing that a test would reveal that something was wrong with one of them so they could put a finger on it, treat it, or at least know exactly what was preventing them from having a child, but they were left playing the waiting game.

I've never fully understood barrenness in the Bible. It seems that every woman who is said to be barren ends up having a miracle baby. Think about it—Sarah, Rebekah, Rachel, Hannah, Elizabeth—they are all without children, and a few of them already qualify for the senior discount at Luby's. Then, lo and behold, they each get pregnant and have a miracle child. It's almost as if the reason barrenness is even mentioned is to set off signals that God is about to show up and perform something miraculous. Infertility in Scripture carries with it this sign that says, "Behold! A baby will be delivered from this barren womb." The only exception is Michal from 2 Samuel 6:23: "And Michal daughter of Saul had no children to the day of her death." Some interpret that to mean that God closed her womb. I interpret that to mean that it didn't happen anymore between her and David. After all, when you have multiple wives like David did, it's not like you're sexually starving. David cut her off.

I wish there was a story in Scripture about a woman whose womb was empty and ended up dying, having never experienced the pains of childbirth. It's not that I'd wish anything like this on a woman, but it would give barren women today someone to connect with. It would give them a close friend and companion, someone who felt their pain to the core of her being. Why should godly women in Christ-centered marriages not have children while fourteen-year-olds who get in the back of a Jeep with someone on the first date get pregnant?

At times, barrenness got the best of Jenny. She battled with depression and wrestled with God over this for years. Her simple request was for her womb to bear fruit. In 2009, she sat us down to share what she had learned from the Lord while in a season of searching for answers and meaning in regard to her status. She said that she had come to peace with her infertility. She didn't want people walking by her casket saying, "Look. There's that poor infertile woman." She wanted them to say, "Look, there's a woman who continued to serve the Lord even when she didn't get her way."

Jenny valued Malaya too much to allow her emptiness to result in neglect of any kind. In fact, on Jenny's thirty-first birthday, in a room full of women gathered together to bless and pray over her, she spoke this over Malaya: "Malaya—you're snazzy; you stand up for yourself, love God, love your family and friends, love reading your Bible. You have a desire for everyone to know Jesus and a compassionate spirit. You are my greatest gift and most special thing to celebrate! When you were born was when I learned what prayer truly meant! I knew I had to have it to be the mama that you deserved!"

After Jenny had Malaya, she was eager to have more children. It wasn't because Malaya wasn't enough, but that life with her had proven to be so precious and sweet, she wanted more.

There were moments when the waiting room was so crowded that security came and asked people to leave. All of our friends didn't leave; they just went to the other waiting rooms throughout the hospital. Every time we received news about Jenny, a runner would take the news from one waiting area to another. It was like the mother church had birthed church plants all over Baylor Grapevine hospital. Denominational lines didn't matter. People from all branches of Christianity held hands believing in the God of healing. It was church—the body of Christ—at its best.

Music played in Jenny's room around the clock, and at the end of each day, doctors and nurses were singing along with the lyrics of songs they had never heard before. A couple of songs that sustained us were "Mighty to Save" and "Healer" by Hillsong.

David, Jenny's husband of eleven years, stood by her side, reading every Facebook message, every text, every email—word for word—over her still body. His voice began to fade as he continued reading night and day. His wife was battling for her life, and this became his way of extending covenant love.

I could walk you through the hospital and show you places where my mom hid behind columns crying, where my family sat in rooms with doctors making big decisions, and where our knees became numb as we prayed for hours.

We thought the day they amputated her legs was the worst day of all. Her body fought so hard to protect her organs from septic shock that blood wasn't circulating to her feet or fingertips. But we knew we would take Jenny's life and wit over her legs and fingernails.

The struggle lasted eighteen days. We had been told that there was a one in five hundred thousand chance that sepsis would go to her brain. There was a better chance for Jenny to be struck by lightning in 2010—*twice*—than for the septic shock to go to her brain. On February 22, 2010, we received the news that it had happened. The family was called in to say good-bye.

Family, friends, and even nurses circled Jenny's bed to tell her good-bye. Through the tears, my mom took the lead that day and said, "I need everyone to listen."

Now, my mom is only five foot two. We used to joke that she would gladly take a bullet for any of her children; the only problem was that the bullet could still hit you from the belly button up. But even though she's short, she demands authority when she speaks.

She said, "I need everyone to listen to me. We are not going to bow down to any other gods. We don't like this. We don't agree with it. But we are not going to serve another. Do you hear me? We are not going to bow down and serve any other gods." In the moments when grief intrudes upon one's life, other "gods" (or idols) show up in an attempt to take up residence. They come in the form of self-reliance, depression, entitlement, and permanent expressions of bitterness. Somehow, my mother felt compelled to rebuke these idols. And she proceeded to go around the circle of friends that day, and each person who was present agreed to this covenant, even the nurses.

After my brother-in-law removed a lock of Jenny's hair, my family was excused from the room because the doctors said it could sometimes be a disturbing scene. As Jenny breathed her last breath, a doctor sang the ancient hymn that seems to transcend the ages, "It Is Well," over her body: "It is well,/With my soul./It is well, it is well, with my soul."

David lost his wife. Malaya lost her mom. My parents lost their only daughter. Jonathan and I lost our sister. The world lost a friend and a devout follower of Jesus.

Why would God remain silent or choose to ignore the petitions of what ended up being over fifteen thousand prayer warriors?

Why do we read verses in the New Testament that make prayer seem so easy?

Ask and it will be given to you; seek and you will find; knock and the door will be opened to you.
For everyone who asks receives; those who seek find, and to those who knock, the door will be opened.[2]

. . . Whatever you ask for in prayer, believe that you have received it, and it will be yours.[3]

If you remain in me and my words remain in you, ask for whatever you wish, and it will be done for you.[4]

Is calling God into action about getting the formula right? Because we tried.

Is it about faith? If so, did we lack it?

We had people throughout Jenny's eighteen-day struggle who told us about dreams they had received about Jenny being healed. We had people who told us to just name it and claim it. "Name the healing for what it needs to be," they would say, "and then claim it done in the name of Jesus."

But what about when healing doesn't come? How damaging is it to someone's soul when they are told that if they pray in faith it will be done, yet something isn't done? Does that mean their faith wasn't strong enough? Does it mean they didn't pray hard enough? Does it mean there was a bad connection in the prayer line?

Or could it be that Jesus didn't come to heal the world of disease? Could it be that he came to invite people into an adventure that would be littered with sickness, illness, and even death? If Jesus came to heal the world of disease, he failed. It hit me. Every person Jesus healed, at some point in that person's life, got sick again. Even the people Jesus brought back to life, at some point, died again.

It's interesting that Jesus goes to the pool called Bethesda in John 5. It's a place where a lot of disabled people hung out, hoping they would be the first to jump into the water when it stirred and be healed. The fact that Jesus goes to the pool tells you something about him. He goes to a place where outcasts and social misfits hung out. He knew what he was walking into.

Jesus left the scene having only healed one person. *One person.* A pool full of sick people, and he heals one. Am I the only one who finds that to be strange?

My dad tells the story of walking out of the hospital with my mom, knowing that at the age of fifty-three and fifty-two they had outlived their oldest child. They approached the sliding glass doors leading not just to a parking lot, but to a life they had never known before. There would not be a "normal" anymore. They each walked with a limp, because the lifelong journey of grief was setting in. My mom looked at my dad and said, "Remind me what we believe. What do we believe?"

After a few moments, my dad responded with these words: "The tomb is empty. The tomb is empty."

3

WALKING WITH A LIMP

We live with grief. Life doesn't turn out the way we expect, and we suffer the loss. The health we expected into old age is suddenly lost. The child we thought was "normal" turns out to have special challenges. The teenager we love more than life makes destructive choices. The job we worked hard for is suddenly lost in a down-sized economy. The marriage we thought was perfect turns out to be wearisome. The one we love so much dies. . . . The years roll by and grief changes. But it doesn't leave. And sometimes it sneaks up and bites us unexpectedly. . . . What I've learned about grief, though, is this: it's the only way. I can't ignore it; I can't set it aside; I can't pretend. I must grieve my way through the sorrow and the loss. Painful as it is, grief is a gift—a part of the healing process.

—MIKE COPE [1]

When two brothers in their late twenties are together, they should be doing something like enjoying a basketball game or eating wings while watching football—not doing a funeral for their thirty-one-year-old sister.

I've been amazed to see Jonathan's gift of leading worship develop over the last decade, but I've never seen him as anointed as he was on February 25, 2010. The solo he sang of Leonard Cohen's "Hallelujah" was absolutely mesmerizing.

After Jesse Beebe—Jenny's best friend and founder of Kidstand,[2] a ministry Jenny was highly involved in—spoke a few words and prayed a powerful prayer about hope, I got up to speak, not knowing if words were going to come out of my mouth. The joke during the hospital stay was that the Ross family hadn't cried this hard since *The Fresh Prince of Bel-Air* went off the air back in 1996. Don't laugh; it was a traumatic day for my family. We used to reenact *Fresh Prince* scenes at the dinner table.

But that day in The Hills Church of Christ sanctuary, I stood, not sure if I'd have the strength to speak a word. I wasn't sure if I'd even be able to walk again, because I felt so weak. We were a crippled family. Grief will do that to you. It will leave you staggering through life.

I stood holding a microphone, and all I knew to do was to open my mouth and pray for God to speak a word. I was struck with the reality that this crippling feeling is here to stay for a while. It's not leaving. Like a newborn child, grievers begin as infants and must learn to walk again, even though the walk will always be with a limp.

Going into the memorial service, two words wouldn't let me go—"Jesus wins." Even when it seems like death has won, the story of Easter echoes from the empty tomb that death couldn't hold Jesus, and death still can't hold us. Death doesn't get the last word. Jesus wins!

In front of over a thousand people, I remember looking at David, "David, you were a brother before you were a brother-in-law. We couldn't have asked for a man to come into Jenny's life to love her the way you did. We are in this together for life.

"Malaya, you asked me to tell the story about the time your mom broke up with her high school boyfriend and he threw up in the front yard. So there, I told the story. On a serious note, I want you to know that we are going to fight for your faith. We are going to fight for you to know Jesus.

"Mom, your daughter became your best friend. She adored you.

"Dad, you called her your princess. You and Mom raised us to love Jesus. You pointed us to him. And we are going to cling to him today and forever."

I spoke a few words to my uncle and aunt, cousins, grandma, and to David's family. Then, after having everyone kneel, we prayed a prayer of victory. *Jesus wins!*

For so many reasons, I'm drawn to Dr. Martin Luther King Jr.'s life and passion. It's eerie to read the last few words of his speech to striking sanitation workers in Memphis in April 1968:

Like anybody, I would like to live a long life. Longevity
has its place. But I'm not concerned about that now.
I just want to do God's will. And He's allowed me to
go up to the mountain. And I've looked over. And I've
seen the promised land. I may not get there with you.
But I want you to know tonight, that we, as a people,
will get to the promised land. And I'm happy, tonight.
I'm not worried about anything. I'm not fearing any
man. Mine eyes have seen the glory of the coming of
the Lord.[3]

Etched on the brick walls of the National Civil Rights
Museum a few miles from my home are these words. Dr.
King knew his life was hanging by a thread and that the
clock was ticking. When you hear him speak words like "I
may not get there with you," you can't help but sit back in
your recliner and shake your head in amazement.

At Jenny's thirty-first birthday party, she wanted to
take the focus off herself and celebrate the lives of other
women who had impacted her in a variety of ways.

After speaking words of blessing over each of them,
she prayed a prayer that she had written out. Here is the
last paragraph:

I praise you, God, that you have blessed me with this
specific cloud of witnesses!! I am so favored by you for
giving me them! It makes me want to fall back into

your arms and take this huge sigh to know when I die it is many of these girls that will greet me and be the forefront to your glory in Heaven and that maybe they will even be the ones to vocalize to me and step aside to reveal my Savior!! As they beautifully and angelically say, "Jenny, this is Jesus!" And for those that pass after me, it will be such great days in heaven to welcome them in and to give them some of their first heavenly hugs and kisses!

"And for those that pass after me . . ."

I don't know what to make of these words. I also don't know what to make of the fact that Jenny wasn't healed.

I'll probably never know why God didn't heal Jenny. I'll also never know why Jews suffered in the Holocaust, why African-Americans have been stripped of human dignity, why children are molested, why people starve to death while others' pantries are overly stocked, why three-year-olds are sold into slavery in Ghana, and why prosperity is accepted as a sign of God's approval.

I *do* know this: Genesis 3 was an event that did more than damage the human soul. Adam and Eve's decision to step across the boundaries that God set up to protect life—not because he was eager to micromanage all of life, but because he was passionate about protecting and sustaining the goodness of creation—cracked the entire cosmos. All of creation went berserk. In fact, if you read

Genesis 3 literally, only two things were actually cursed: the serpent and the ground. (If I'm the ground, I'm wondering what I did to deserve such punishment.) Because all of creation is intricately linked together, all living things suffer.

In a strange, mystical way, suffering links us with all of creation.

I know that many people in the world have suffered far greater tragedies than I did with my sister. It doesn't dismiss the sting of her death, and it doesn't mean that I don't have the right to grieve. It simply affirms that all of creation bears the scars of a cracked cosmos.

So, what's God up to?

When my sister lost her battle, I couldn't help but ask questions. As I walk the streets of Memphis today, witnessing severe brokenness and pain, questions naturally flow out of my life. I never doubt God's existence, but I have wrestled with doubts about his activity in the world. In fact, this book began as a commitment I made during the season of Lent in 2010 to set aside a few journaling sessions a week to wrestle with the intervention of God. Writing became an outlet for me to personally explore my questions.

Some people choose to become Deists because they sometimes feel like God has taken his hand off the world.

Deism basically says that God created the world, set it in motion, and then stepped back. Then, one day, he will return to make all things right. I just couldn't go there.

When we choose to follow Jesus, there will be moments in our lives when we will ask, "What does it mean to be a disciple when we don't get our way?"

We have a story in John's gospel about some disciples of Jesus who choose to stop following him. John writes, "From this time many of his disciples turned back and no longer followed him."[4] Can you imagine? Here are people who had walked the same roads alongside God-in-the-flesh and had witnessed miracles firsthand, yet they realized that following Jesus might not be all it was cracked up to be.

Jesus asked the Twelve a legitimate question: "You do not want to leave too, do you?"

Simon Peter answered him, "Lord, to whom shall we go?"

For most of my life, I've read that story as if Simon Peter's answer was a no-brainer, as if he were saying, "Are you kidding me? Of course we're not leaving. We're with you until the end."

But now, in light of my experiences, I wonder if his response was more like this: "Jesus, if we had somewhere else to go right now, we might do it, but we have nowhere else to go. We don't know how this story is going to play itself out, but we're in. We're with you. We want to see where this adventure leads us."

■   ■   ■

I can't help but wonder if Matthew writes from a season of grief. After all, most scholars have Matthew writing around the time when the Temple in Jerusalem was destroyed. Jews were being persecuted. Life was rough. Maybe this is why he concludes his story of Jesus with words of hope, not words of commissioning. The last sentence, "I am with you always," was carefully chosen. Matthew wanted to leave his readers with a promise that God's presence is thick even in the midst of chaos.

And this promise—a promise of God's abiding presence—keeps me seeking even in my confusion, pain, and grief.

BEING A DISCIPLE WHEN WE DON'T GET OUR WAY

I do not at all understand the mystery of grace—only that it meets us where we are but does not leave us where it found us. It can be received gladly or grudgingly, in big gulps or in tiny tastes, like a deer at the salt. I gobbled it, licked it, held it down between my little hooves.

—ANNE LAMOTT [1]

We grieve hard because we love hard.

Sometimes people use the image found in James describing life as a mist—one moment you are here, and the next moment you are gone. There is truth that life happens within a very short time. For some, it's shorter than others. But I'm not sure God looks upon human life as a mist. I don't think God wants the image of a vapor to be the defining image of someone's life. He created us with a hunger for joy, passion, and purpose. He created us for relationship. He created us to be a part of heaven on earth.

During Jenny's eighteen-day struggle, we had a daily journal going on CarePages—a Web service that enables friends and family of patients to remain connected. The encouragement we received during those two weeks, and even a few weeks afterward, was overwhelming. A Care-Pages community had been birthed. People who didn't even know Jenny drove over four hours to attend Jenny's memorial service. They simply got caught up in the story.

We continued journaling a few weeks after Jenny's death to inform CarePages followers of fund-raisers and to give updates from the grief journey. Old and new friends grieved with us, and an additional two thousand joined the CarePages community after Jenny died. They kept reading, so we kept writing.

Three weeks after Jenny's death, the family posted a song written from the valley of Jenny's fight for her life. The lyrics spurred controversy, and the interest in post-ing updates about the grief journey came to a screeching halt because we didn't have the energy to enter into such theological dialogues.

Grief includes a lot more than death. We grieve be-cause of divorce, cancer, kids who go astray, loss of jobs, and the list could go on. There are moments when the griever is eager to hear a word of encouragement, hope, and even advice. However, it becomes dangerous when the friends of grievers feel like they need to *do* theology in-stead of just trying to *be* theology. In other words, people begin to describe why the event happened, and unknowingly they attempt to manipulate the griever instead of offering a ministry of presence: "I'm just here to be with you, because I want you to know I care." Job's friends were great companions until they opened their mouths.

This song wasn't written weeks or months after the event in an attempt to reflect upon the struggle. It was written in the midst of the pain. It ministered to us, and we posted it.

Some Explaining to Do
by Lisa Aschmann and Karen Taylor-Good

Her faith was like a river, it ran so strong and wild
She was full of love and promise, and she was Your child
So why'd she have to suffer when she loved You so well
You must have had a reason . . . do tell

God, You've got some explaining to do
I'm not saying I'm over believing in You
But when I take my last breath and my life here is through
God, You've got some explaining to do

I believe that someday we'll have a heart to heart
We'll all sit down together, You'll illuminate each part
And I'll say . . . "Oh, I get it, she was living out Your Plan"
But now it just seems mean, like we're Play-Doh in
*   Your hands*

God . . . You've got some explaining to do
I'm not saying I'm over believing in You
But when I take my last breath and my life here is through
God . . . You've got some explaining to do

Cancer and Columbine, earthquakes and tsunamis
Children who are starving 'cause land mines kill their mommies
I swear from this perspective it sure looks hit or miss
I can hardly wait to understand all this

God . . . You've got some explaining to do
I'm not saying I'm over believing in You
But when I take my last breath and my life here is through

I hope to understand the gain that lies behind the grief and pain
I hope to hear in Your own words the reasoning for what occurred
I hope to have more than a hint of what this was and what it meant
I still believe in Your great works but God this really hurts
God, You've got some explaining to do

Written in loving memory of Jenny B.[2]

Reading this song from a cushiony desk chair removed from the tragedy of an event might evoke a different response than reading it in an ICU room while hovering over a sick child inundated with tubes and wires, kept alive only by a breathing machine.

Interpreting words while *in* an event isn't the same as interpreting words *reflecting back* on an event. This is what makes the Psalms so relevant and inviting. They aren't written by heartless musicians eager to meet a recording deadline. Instead, they are written by people who are facing real-life events. This is what makes them raw and tangible.

Anyone can make songs out of the words from Psalm 139:14, "I praise you because I am fearfully and wonderfully made," or Psalm 149:1, "Praise the Lord! Sing to the Lord a new song." These are any songwriter's playing field. But we struggle with the psalms that express doubt, confusion, and hatred toward enemies. Just consider the fact that 40 percent of the Book of Psalms comprises songs of lament. Only 3 percent of the songs in our hymnbooks fit within this genre.

Too many Christian leaders attempt to infuse worship only with exuberant joy. Worship leaders and preachers need to also honor the voice of lament. After all, there are more lament psalms than any other genre of psalms. The psalms—the songs sung by Jesus and early Christ followers—are thick with questions like "How long, O Lord?"

Even Jesus sings a verse of a dark song taught to him by his faith community: "My God, my God, why have you forsaken me?"

When the voice of lament is strangled in our worship gatherings, hearts are ignored. When is the last time you've participated in a Mother's Day or Father's Day that actually honored those who grieve because it's a day that reminds them of death, loss, abuse, absence, or betrayal? Not everyone has a mother to give a rose to, and not everyone has a father they can (or want to) contact.

When was the last time you were told to bring your baggage and pain into a worship gathering instead of leaving it at the door so the congregation could praise the Lord together? Maybe we force others into celebratory moods when many need to know that God can meet them where they are.

When was the last time you were allowed, permitted, or even encouraged to voice that life hurts, it stings, it is painful, and right now it just doesn't seem fair?

Adventures are full of sufferings. The health-and-wealth gospel—which depicts God as one who rewards the righteous with material things—that airs on TV and invades Christian bookstores just doesn't line up with the Jesus we read about in the New Testament. Yes, Jesus is on record saying, "Truly I tell you . . . no one who has left home or wife or brothers or sisters or parents or children for the sake of the kingdom of God will fail to receive many times as much in this age, and in the age to come eternal life." [3] However, which of the disciples went on to file taxes as an upper-class citizen? Which one was exempt from pain? History tells us that they all died the deaths of martyrs. Maybe Jesus had something else in mind. Maybe Jesus was fully aware that life with him would guarantee scars. But scars carry stories. And the stories bear witness to the fact that we've been on a journey. We've been with Jesus. We are people on the move.

Our culture often associates good health with God's favor. The fewer the blemishes and bruises the better. We're quick to cover up scars, except when high school football players wear turf burns as chick magnets, or unless you're a cheek-scarred Tina Fey who has the gift of making people laugh every time you open your mouth. However, Christ followers have chosen to seek after a scar-worn Messiah. Who wants to follow a Messiah who's had no experience walking through the fire? And with Jesus, they're not just scars from the thorns, whips, and nails. They're scars from a reputation that was challenged, verbal abuse that was unwarranted, an apostle named Judas who betrayed him, and disciples who chose to abort the mission.

Have you ever stopped to think why Jesus had scars when he rose from the dead? God could have healed the scars. He could have made Jesus whole. But instead we have a story of a risen Lord whose scars tell a story. I wonder if Jesus will still bear the scars when God redeems all things. Will the scars still bear witness?

When the disciples saw Jesus' scars, their passion for him increased significantly. I've been encouraged to search for mentors, ministers, and leaders who bear scars because they have lived life. My good friend and mentor, Mike Cope, has told me on a number of occasions that few people have ministered to him who haven't endured deep forms of suffering.

My brother-in-law, David Bizaillion, one who was a brother to me and Jonathan before he was a brother-in-law, continues to grieve hard. A few weeks after Jenny's death, he told me that he has had moments when he simply wanted to give God the finger and walk away. In the moment, he wasn't attempting to be blasphemous; he was being honest. I've known people who have described grief as shaking a fist at God. For them and for David, it's not because they want to give up on God; it's because they know that God can do more than they could ever ask or imagine.

I think the Bible allows and permits questions, concerns, and even doubts. In fact, that's often how our faith is strengthened. One friend mentioned that faith isn't the absence of doubt; it's the absence of certainty. I think this is why Jesus was more prone to ask good questions than he was to give people all the right answers. Jesus modeled honesty within the moment, and we see this when he was in the garden, knowing a brutal death knocked at the door and praying for the cup to be taken from him. Nailed to a cross, he sang the song about being forsaken by God from Psalm 22. There's this sense of mystery that somehow, even in that tragic moment, God's presence was thick.

A few months after Jenny's death, one of my good friends who's a preacher in north Dallas, Chris Seidman, watched his oldest son battle infections in the hospital for nearly two months. The doctors were baffled, but eleven-year-old Skyler kept fighting.

Chris and Tara, two faithful Jesus followers and prayer warriors, spent day and night praying and reading Scripture over Skyler. One night, Skyler looked up at his dad and said, "Why me?" In that moment, Chris gave his son permission to tell God exactly how he felt.

He would later tweet:

Sky update - No relief 4 rash. By far, darkest non-life threatening day these 45 days. Sky's in a rage. Told him he could let God have it. Been beside him as he's been hollering @ God. If any concerned w/ my counsel, I suggest they read psalms. God can handle it.

■　　■　　■

Three months after Jenny's death, I was able to journal a much-needed letter to God. I felt covered in his grace, and I desperately laid my soul before him in its entirety.

God,

I've been meaning to write this letter for a while now. It has been stirring within my mind for nearly three months. Some phrases, expressions, and emotions have been long forgotten (though I vowed to write them down) while others linger as fresh as they were during the eighteen days of hell I endured back in February.

I have been changed because of this traumatic experience. My theology has been challenged. My heart has been broken. My confidence in you has been strangled. I have so many questions, concerns, and frustrations.

For nearly eighteen days, thousands of people begged for Jenny's healing. A few days we were given thin glimpses of what seemed to be divine movements that could only be described as miracles. Even the doctors were using phrases like "Things are happening that we are unable to explain." Plummeting blood pressure went back up. A swollen gallbladder had CT scans revealing nothing less than normal. Pulses were found in black hands and feet, signifying that life was in what seemed to be death. We petitioned you from hallways, bedsides, waiting rooms, elevators, chapels, cars, restaurants, and bathrooms. The ground of the earth was covered with the footprints of people who were begging for Jenny's life.

For eighteen days, we prayed the hell out of everywhere we were.

What happened? What are we left to believe?

God, I'm angry because I think the world of you. I'm not angry because I doubt your presence; I'm ticked off because I'm convinced that your presence was with us and you were there with the power to breathe life and you didn't. All it would take was one word from your lips. The same tongue that spoke, "Light!" and there was light, could have spoken a word and blood would have flowed, septic shock would have fled, blood pressure would have held steady, and limbs would have been made strong.

If we are just pawns in this story, if we are just objects that you want to use to bring you glory, if we are simply agents of glorification because you don't feel like you're getting any . . . then I just want to say, "Forget that story."

Did you tease us with moments when it seemed that healing was knocking at the door and then slipping through the cracks? Why did we have to endure amputated legs and dead fingertips? For eighteen days we were just strung along with glimpses of hope, but in the end we were left with our own set of crippled legs and punctured lungs.

Yet, in spite of all of the questions and confusion, I still believe. I believe in the power of the Resurrection. I've never needed an Easter more than I needed the one on April 4th. I've never needed to preach an Easter sermon more than I needed that one. I've never needed to believe the Easter message more.

I'm convinced now more than ever that death does not get the last word. Death isn't how our story ends, even if it feels like a chaotic story. We win, and the declaration we made toward the end of Jenny's memorial service will stick with me for years to come, as we bowed down on our knees and invited the presence of evil to get a glimpse of this. That even in a moment where it seems like darkness has won, light comes into the darkness as a reminder that darkness never wins. The Jesus story is all about light conquering darkness.

I'm tempted to live with low expectations of you. Because if I choose to live with low expectations, it will be near to impossible for me to ever feel like you have let me down. This could save me from ever feeling the grief and pain of the silence of God. And you know what? Many people choose this route. They choose to believe that you have taken your hands off and that one day you'll make everything right, that you are not actively working in the world now. But the story of Jesus that I'm caught up in encourages me to live with high expectations of you. It causes freakish kinds of convictions to swell up within me declaring that you are active, present, able, and willing. But again, I know that to live with high expectations means that there will be moments where I will feel like you have let me down . . . like you have taken a wrong turn. And I'm just going to have to live with that.

Here's what I love about you . . . here is what keeps me grounded in this story:

1) *<u>You are love</u>. I am convinced at this point in my life that you are driven by love, not a need for glory. If my conviction is true, then I can do something in my life and ministry with a God who chooses to love in the midst of crap. I can hold on to that.*

2) *<u>You choose to enter into chaos</u>. Your track record has a long listing of story after story of your choice to enter into the chaos of life. You don't care for the downtrodden from the outside in, but you enter into the mess with us. This is what makes me want to become a more faithful disciple, because the way of Jesus is absolutely the most ridiculous thing this world has ever seen, because we couldn't imagine a God who would*

enter into human flesh to become it, love it, sit with it, etc. This year, I don't need a God who will lift me out of a ditch, but I need a God who will get down in a ditch with me.

3) *Resurrection. This one word is what keeps me breathing. Your power to conquer the grave has set in motion a new existence. It provides hope in the end, but even more than that, it provides meaning for existence now.*

Thanks for accepting me with all of my emotions, feelings, and questions. Continue to speak into my life.

WHEN GOD GETS LOW

God is not only the God of the sufferers but the God who suffers. The pain and fallenness of humanity have entered into his heart. Through the prism of my tears I have seen a suffering God. . . . And great mystery: to redeem our brokenness and lovelessness the God who suffers with us did not strike some mighty blow of power but sent his beloved son to suffer like us, through his suffering to redeem us from suffering and evil. Instead of explaining our suffering God shares it.

—NICHOLAS WOLTERSTORFF [1]

After speaking at the ACU (Abilene Christian University) Summit in the fall of 2010, my friend and the director of ministry events, Brady Bryce, led me to a table set up on stage where people from all over the world were allowed to email or text questions in order to engage me in dialogue. I'm not much of a Q & A kind of guy. The thought of being asked a question in front of a large crowd that could catch me off guard, leaving me frozen, speechless, baffled—like Eminem choking at the mic in the beginning of *8 Mile*—makes me want to ram my head through a wall. I like to have questions given to me beforehand so I can bounce my answers off a few people before letting loose in front of thousands.

I had just spoken on joy and suffering, and one girl emailed a question. Of all the questions coming at Brady through cyberspace, he decided to ask this one: "Does God cry?"

Does he?

Does God cry?

I grew up singing a song called "No Tears in Heaven," but what about now?

Revelation 21:4 begins by stating that there will be tears in heaven, but that God will wipe them away. The same verse ends declaring that death, mourning, crying, and pain will be no more. But again, what about now?

I wonder why Jesus cried at Lazarus's tomb, even though he knew he was about to raise him from the dead. Maybe he got caught up in the moment. Maybe witnessing his friends grieve was too much to bear. Maybe it was because death always stings, even when you know resurrection is coming.

I wonder why Jesus wept over Jerusalem in Luke 19, knowing that he was about to lay down his life so that people could find life. Was the oppression and injustice too much? Was it because the kind of righteousness God created and desired had been strangled and watered down?

Hebrews displays this side of Jesus with these words: "During the days, Jesus' life on earth, he offered up prayers and petitions with fervent cries and tears to the one who could save him from death, and he was heard because of his reverent submission."[2]

One day, God will make all things new, and heaven will come crashing into the earth as the groans of creation are redeemed. Tears will be wiped away, death will be defeated, and sin will be no more. But until the new heaven and new earth invade our current reality of suffering, tears will continue to flow. So, when towers fall, tornadoes destroy, pregnant women miscarry, husbands break wedding vows, and the innocent die because wars are fueled by a hunger for control and power, the first tear to roll off a cheek is a tear from God.

There are only a few people in this world that I can say I've known all my life. Jenny is one of them. She had just turned two when I was born. With her, there was never sibling rivalry. There was immediate connection. We were siblings who were also friends, or friends who happened to be siblings. The first sixteen years of my life she was the protective one, and we have a number of stories to prove it. If she didn't like a girl I was dating, she was quick to make life miserable for everyone involved.

When I turned sixteen, about the same time she was

settling into college life, the roles reversed. I immediately became the protective brother the first time she used the word *marriage*. It was like she had dropped the f-bomb or something. I was offended by it. It made me nauseated. And I decided to do something about it.

From three hours away I would closely monitor her love life. I was seventeen when she first brought home a guy from college, and I was confident that I could take out some punk kid from Abilene Christian University who tried to make a move on her. After all, Jonathan and I watched *WWF Monday Night Raw* every week, and I'd seen *Karate Kid*, like, five times.

She contacted us one night to tell us that she was bringing a boy home to meet the family, and I was determined not to like him. I wore the tightest shirt I could find and did bicep curls before "the moment" arrived just to add to the intimidation factor. This guy walked into the room. My arms were crossed and I was ready to destroy anything that even looked at my sister in a flirtatious manner when his first words hit me: "Hey, Josh, I hear you're a pretty good football player." If he had started with "Hey, Josh, I'm David," I probably would have refused the handshake and given him the eye, but when he started with a compliment, I gave in. He's been part of the fam ever since, and I couldn't ask for a better brother-in-law.

▪   ▪   ▪

As we sat in the ICU waiting room, twenty-nine years of memories flooded my mind. I'd heard about the transforming power of ICU waiting rooms. I'd sat in a number of them in my eight to nine years of ministry, but it was different this time.

Waiting rooms force you to ask questions that you don't ask in the real world.

I'd wrestled with the activity of God and spiritual warfare before, but it took on a new meaning in a place like this.

I attempted to pray through the Beattitudes in Matthew 5 regularly, words from Jesus that include "Blessed are those who mourn, for they will be comforted," but they spoke to my soul in a different way this time.

I had preached on the power of community quite often, but I felt its power like never before in the waiting room.

I was a changed man because of this brutal illness in Jenny, and I trusted it was a good thing. But at one point, I needed something different from God. I needed God to cry with me, and he did.

Some people think that God doesn't cry because he doesn't have any emotions. This just doesn't sound to me like the God who hung out in the Judean countryside.

If you think that God doesn't have emotions, then you serve a God who stands at a distance, and that can be dangerous to your spiritual journey.

I looked around the waiting room, and I saw a place

that had been bathed in tears. We had cried on chairs, against walls, leaning on Coke machines, and standing in circles while praying. And, God joined us here.

I love the way Matthew concluded his gospel declaring that our story is one where Jesus is present with people. He abides. He hangs out. He enters into pain. He cries with us.

I've come to believe that God is more horizontal than vertical. I used to believe that God was over us, hovering in the sky like an outer-space satellite, occasionally sticking his finger into the world, but mostly in the position of a life guard on duty. Jesus has led me to believe that God isn't just *over* the world, but that he's *in* the world.

For our last project in seminary, my professor had us write a short paper on our metaphor of ministry. It was a fun paper meant to invoke creativity. One guy described ministry as a golf caddie, another as an orchestra conductors, and yet another wrote about being a UFC fighter (a metaphor that didn't get him a good grade, but surely we've all been tempted to put church people in choke holds before).

I chose the image of a crossing guard. At the time, the only thing separating the home where my wife Kayci and I lived from an elementary school was a four-way stop. Every day—in heat, snow, rain, sleet—the crossing guard was present. Here's what caught my attention: she never stood on the opposite side of the road from the children, saying to them, "Come on over." Neither did she stand on the same side with the kids, signaling them to go ahead when it looked clear. Instead, she held her stop sign and walked *with* the kids through the intersection.

I understand that every metaphor breaks down at some point, but for me, this wasn't just a metaphor to describe ministry. It was an accurate portrayal of Jesus' life and ministry. Jesus doesn't stand on the other side of life, waving us over when the coast is clear. Likewise, he doesn't stand next to us, patting us on the back and wishing us good luck as we trudge through life.

The story of the good news of Jesus is that he enters.

He enters.

He enters into the world.

He enters into human flesh.

He enters into the suffering of people.

He enters into the brokenness of life.

He enters into all forms of pain.

He enters into the margins.

John declared, "The Word became flesh and made his dwelling among us."[3] In *The Message*, Eugene Peterson gave it this twist: "The Word became flesh and blood, and moved into the neighborhood."

It does something to my soul to know that when I feel like I'm as low as I can get, God's grace can get lower. I'm encouraged to know that when we read in Exodus 2 that

God showed up to deliver his people, we discover phrases such as "God heard their groaning," and "God looked on them."[4] I'm equally blown away that Jesus "made himself nothing by taking the very nature of a servant."[5] God stoops low.

God often chooses the path of *descent* instead of the path of *ascent.* He descends into the world with relationship and redemption on his mind. He's not just throwing life preservers into the water to pull people to safety, he's jumping into the messes of life, eager to unleash his acts of redemption.

Quite honestly, there are days when I don't need a God who will deliver me from the pit, just a God who will get down in a pit with me.

I was with a man recently who confessed the sin of pornography, fantasizing, and masturbation. He described his faith as a ladder. He kept trying to climb it to get to God, but he kept falling. He was guilt-ridden and disturbed that he couldn't climb the ladder. I said, "Don't miss the good news of God. We don't have to climb a ladder to him. He has climbed down a ladder to get to us."

My affections have grown for the man who walked the Judean countryside interacting with the have-nots of his day. Jesus has captured my heart because of his treatment toward the least of these.

Luke 5 comes to mind. It tells of the moment when Jesus was approached by a man with leprosy. In the first century, if you had a skin disease, you weren't allowed to enter within a certain radius of other humans. In fact, the law of isolation from Leviticus 13:45–46 prevented you from doing this. Develop a skin disease, and you might not touch your wife's face or your kids' hands again. It was more than a physical disease; it was a social disease. So, in this story, the man with leprosy seemed to break the law of isolation.

However, a closer look at the story will reveal that someone else was actually the lawbreaker. Someone else touched the man with leprosy, therefore becoming unclean. That somebody was Jesus. He could have spoken the word that would have healed the disease. He could have told the man to bathe in the nearest lake or river. He could have said that he'd pray for him. Instead, Jesus touched the man. Before healing his physical disease, Jesus healed his social disease by entering into his suffering. Jesus became unclean.

Jesus had respect for the law, yet he also came to help people interpret the law correctly. Leviticus is very clear about who is clean and who is not clean. I'm not sure if any book in the Bible holds more responsibility for killing the New Year's goal of reading through the entire Bible in one year than Leviticus. Genesis and Exodus are smooth sailing, but once people begin "begetting" one after another, and others have to go through cleaning rituals because they accidently touched a carcass, or a man is unable to sit in a chair if his bleeding wife sat there, many readers don't have the patience to make it to the next book. And if they do, Numbers might sever the final thread someone is hanging on to.

One thing is sure, Leviticus is very clear that people who have been among the dead and women who are bleeding are unclean. They can't touch, and they can't be touched. Yet, three stories in Luke 8 depict Jesus becoming unclean. The law must be interpreted through the overarching story of God—he cares about dignity, status, and injustice. God stoops to restore the broken to their rightful identities as image bearers of the Almighty.

When I was preaching in Houston, a woman came to the office one day. She had been homeless for years and would come by the office to pick up her mail; her address was the church's address. I was preparing to preach a sermon from Luke 5:12–16 about Jesus touching the man with leprosy, and I was in my office praying for God to teach me what it meant to love the unlovable and touch the untouchable.

While I sat with my pen in one hand and a commentary in the other, Nikki rang the doorbell at the church. This day, she wasn't coming for her mail but for food. I walked with her to the nearest convenience store to get her a bag of peanut butter crackers, some fruit bars, and a couple bottles of water. As I entered the store, I felt this strong conviction that I needed to put my hand on Nikki's shoulder to bless her. Needless to say, I didn't say yes right away.

You see, Nikki had developed awful hygiene. If you were within a fifty-foot radius of her you could smell her. If you took Nikki in your vehicle to get a bite to eat or to drop her off at a motel so she could get a shower, your vehicle would stink for days, if not weeks. Year-round in Houston, Texas, even in the six months of brutal heat, Nikki wore sweatpants and a sweatshirt for weeks at a time without ever washing her clothing.

I was bargaining with God, asking him for a compromise. "Come on, God, how about a fist bump, and we can even blow it up at the end?" The conviction only got stronger, so despite my own hang-ups, I decided to act in obedience.

I walked outside and handed her a bag of purchased items. As she took the bag, I placed my hand on her shoulder, and I blessed her in the name of Jesus. I could feel the heat and sweat coming off her body, but I quickly forgot about the stench when I saw her smile. Come to find out, it had been weeks since she had been touched by a human being.

Maybe that touch was for her that day. Maybe it was for me as a way to introduce me to Jesus, the one who willingly chose to enter into the sufferings of people. Maybe lessons about the power of Jesus' touch are what have carried me through seasons of grief and brokenness.

Is this how suffering works? Is it that no matter what the outcome is—even if we're left with severe scars that we'll carry for the rest of our lives like pictures in a photo album that we can't erase—that God enters into the story? Is that enough?

For some, these are the questions that destroy faith. For others, they are the questions that strengthen faith.

When loved ones die, people say bizarre things:

- God just needed another angel.
- God needed Jenny more than we did.
- Just be happy. She's in a better place.
- Were you really close to her? You rarely mentioned her in your sermons.
- God was protecting her from something that was going to happen later in life.
- If Jenny had a decision to come back right now, she wouldn't want to.

I was prepared to offer grace, because most people meant well. For those who threw out these ridiculous platitudes, I wanted to respond with one statement: "Tell that to a nine-year-old daughter who just lost her mom, and see if she wants to follow that God." But I didn't. I knew people were only trying to offer words of healing.

I spoke at a couple of conferences within the first few months after Jenny died. A mentor and friend, Randy Harris, was at both events, and he became a sounding board for all of my questions, concerns, and doubts. Over chips and salsa, he listened to my struggles. In Malibu, California, I was asking all kinds of questions about Jesus, pain, and where God is in the midst of suffering. I couldn't help but bring up Malaya. It didn't make sense that God would allow the mother of a young girl to die.

Randy said, "Josh, let me hold your hand while I say this." With that he grabbed my left hand with both of his. "Why should Malaya not have to bear part of the suffering of the world?" In other words, all of creation is groaning for redemption. This isn't my song, and it's not Malaya's song. It's our song. It's the song of humanity. It's the song of creation.

That statement opened me up to a greater understanding of the suffering going on all around me. For years I'd been sensitive to it, but that became a defining moment for me in the grieving process. The call of God was for me to follow Jesus now into places of suffering.

Yet this question lingered: Do I still want to follow Jesus into these places?

PART 2

LIVING WITH SCARS

The problem is, many of the people in need of saving are in churches, and at least part of what they need saving from is the idea that God sees the world the same way they do. What if the gravel of a parking lot looks as promising to God as the floorboards of a church? What if a lost soul strikes God as more reachable than a lifelong believer? What if God can drop a ladder absolutely anywhere, with no regard for the religious standards developed by those who have made it their business to know the way to God?

—BARBARA BROWN TAYLOR [1]

INITIATED INTO UNDESIRED CLUBS

The darkness is so dark—and I am alone.—Unwanted, forsaken.—The loneliness of the heart that wants love is unbearable.—Where is my faith?—even deep down, right in, there is nothing but emptiness & darkness.—My God—how painful is this unknown pain. It pains without ceasing.—I have no faith.—I dare not utter the words & thoughts that crowd in my heart—& make me suffer untold agony. So many unanswered questions live within me—I am afraid to uncover them—because of the blasphemy—If there be God,—please forgive me.—Trust that all will end in Heaven with Jesus.

—MOTHER TERESA [1]

I've caused my fair share of suffering in my life. I regret breaking up with my seventh grade girlfriend on Valentine's Day, but I was insensitive, immature, and cheap. I knew I would get grounded by talking my brother into drinking Worcestershire sauce when he was young, but it was before I cared about praying for God to "lead me not into temptation." I just didn't know his lips would swell like they did.

In my thirty-two years of driving, I've only been the cause of one car accident. It was a Sunday afternoon, and my youth group friends chose to play softball in the mud. We were sixteen- and seventeen-year-old boys who were diving into bases we had no business diving into. The problem was, at that age, we didn't do a very good job of thinking ahead. Most of us were driving our parents' vehicles. For me, it was my dad's brand-new 1995 Ford Ranger. I was fully aware that I only had a ten-minute drive home, so I proceeded to put my muddy sweatpants and sweatshirt in the bed of the truck. It was me at the steering wheel in nothing but my boxer shorts and flip-flops.

About halfway home, I got stuck in traffic. I could see over a bridge that there had been a wreck, so I began to do what many people do when there's a wreck: I stretched as high as I could to see what had happened. That's when I failed to see that the car in front of me had put on his breaks. It wasn't a terrible crash. I was only going 10 or 15 miles per hour, but after stepping out of his vehicle, he motioned for me to get out of my truck and I nervously shook my head no at first. Hesitantly, knowing that I had to eventually get out to assess the damage, I opened the door and walked toward the man I had just rear-ended. That's when the cars around me began honking their horns and yelling unkind things out their windows.

The most embarrassing component of the story wasn't that I was standing in the middle of traffic in Mesquite, Texas, wearing nothing but my boxers; it's that for some unknown reason I had chosen to wear tight *Snow White and the Seven Dwarfs* boxers that day. When the man saw my attire, his eyes got big, and then he said, "I've been rear-ended before." He got in his car and drove off. It's a miracle that I ever recovered emotionally from that moment.

I may have only been the cause of one car accident, but regrettably, I've caused plenty of emotional and verbal wrecks. I've acted in ways that have left people wounded and scarred. I've also lived life with others in ways that have introduced me to all forms of suffering.

Jenny's sickness and death weren't my first entrance into a suffering world. I haven't known suffering like surviving genocide or famine, but I am familiar with pain. I lost one granddad at the age of fifteen and another when I was twenty-seven. I've experienced the grief from tragic car accidents that took the lives of friends. My vocation as a pastor has led me into hospital rooms among the dying; into countless conversations with people suffering from abortion, divorce, and sexual abuse; into counseling sessions with parents whose children have gone wild; into confessions of guilt from poor decisions made decades ago; and into discussions with people experiencing faith crises due to trauma, skepticism, mismanaged expectations, and destroyed trust. I've stepped into depressed neighborhoods where I've walked alongside America's poorest of the poor and into affluent neighborhoods where I've witnessed the choking thorns of the lure of wealth.

I'm not an expert on suffering, but here's one thing I've learned in my short life: everyone will suffer. It's not a matter of *if* you will suffer, but *when* and *how* you will suffer. I know it is a risk to force suffering into categories, but here's my feeble attempt to sort it into a few different forms.

Intentional Suffering Because We Make Poor Decisions

I walked into the hospital one day to visit Mark. I had received a phone call that he was in the ICU because of a breathing problem. Our church had poured money, time, and resources into Mark and his family. He was a man trying hard to get on his feet. His health problems were keeping him from sustaining a job, which meant that his family was pinching pennies. There were three adults and three children living in a small two-bedroom apartment. I'll never forget the Wednesday night they showed up at church and their thirteen-year-old son began sharing a story with me of how he had watched a shoot-out in his apartment complex from his balcony. Stunned at the sound of gunfire, he remained by the rail as if he were paralyzed, and he witnessed two men shot to death. They were images graven into his memory for life.

I arrived in the ICU and found Mark alone. His relatives had left for food and rest. I began probing, and it turned out he was in the ICU because his lungs were full of weed. Tears streamed down his cheeks as he confessed to using money on marijuana instead of food and clothes for his family.

When decisions are made to neglect the daily needs of relatives in order to feed addictions, people suffer. When people are overcome with a passion to sleep with a colleague because of an emotional affair, the moment of pleasure lasts a few minutes, and then what? These are decisions that destroy marriages and scar children. Get behind a wheel after having four beers, and destructive things can happen. Our sin—our poor choices—scar the world. We continue the story of the fall. Genesis 3 isn't the story of something that *happened*; it's the story of something that *continues to happen.*

I think when God talks about punishing "the children and their children for the sin of the parents to the third and fourth generation,"[2] it's not that he's handing out stomach flu to an eight-year-old because their great-great-grandpa ran a stoplight ninety-two years earlier. I think it's because sinful decisions lead to destruction, and these are the kinds of things that form and shape behavioral patterns. We often worry, are stressed, lie, and cheat because we learned how to do these things from influential people in our lives.

Poor decisions driven by greed, pleasure, and selfishness do not create a world of peace, unity, and harmony. Instead, they leave a world deeply wounded and scarred.

Intentional Suffering Because We Decide to Enter into Brokenness

I've also learned that sometimes people suffer as intentional participants. They aren't innocent bystanders; they are people who enter into broken places because they believe that's the meaning of following Jesus and being a good human being. This is what captured, motivated, and inspired people like Dorothy Day, Mother Teresa, Shane Claiborne, Dr. King, and even Mohandas Gandhi. When Dr. King completed his doctoral degree, he and Coretta were faced with a decision between pastoring a church in Michigan or Alabama. Both were great opportunities, and there was a part of them that wanted to get away from the South, but their hearts were compelled to enter into the fight instead of running from it.

I was only in Memphis a few months when I first ran into Pastor James Williams. We met at the Bent Tree Apartments. It's interesting how he became a part of that community. Before he was *pastor* Williams he was *banker* Williams. During the week he worked in a bank, and on the weekend he preached at a small congregation in Memphis. He developed a heart for children at the Bent Tree apartment complex close to the Memphis International Airport. Bent Tree is a complex most Memphis police officers are familiar with. One officer has stories of being shot at upon first entering Bent Tree. Windows with bullet holes, the smell of gunfire, and outlines with white chalk have become all too familiar in this place. From the outside, the bricks are old, some windows are boarded up, and it looks rugged. On the inside, cycles are being broken.

Williams and his wife, Sandra, began tutoring children in the main lobby of Bent Tree. For him, it was an act of charity. For his wife, it became a passion and a calling. One day, she told him, "I'm going to quit my job so I can pour more time and energy into the kids." He was hesitant about the idea until she began to use his words against him.

"Every Sunday you stand up in front of your church talking about stepping out in faith believing that God will take care of you. Now, let's put it into practice." After a few months, the apartment manager approached them with the news that ever since they had been at Bent Tree, the children's grades had improved and crime had decreased. In response, he decided to give the Williamses an apartment to tutor in for free. It was an answer to prayer, because they had outgrown the lobby.

Their presence in the community had such a major impact that they soon outgrew the apartment. The manager approached Pastor Williams and said, "There's a problem. There are too many kids coming into the apartment to be tutored."

Pastor Williams responded, "That *is* a problem. I can either turn kids away or you can give me another apartment."

The manager proceeded to give them two additional apartments, and today there are three connected apartments being used to tutor children. The first of these children have matured into teenagers who have gone on to graduate from high school with honors. They have been given hope in life. Their dignity has been restored.

Today, in the middle of Bent Tree, you will find a double-wide trailer that now functions as Pastor Williams's church. Having three apartments wasn't enough.

Pastor and Mrs. Williams chose to pour their time and energy into a place many people had written off as hopeless and depressed. When God looks upon places like Bent Tree, the sign he's eager to place on the front gate isn't KEEP OUT or BEWARE. Through Jesus, it is ENGAGE WITH COURAGE because God's love penetrates with purpose.

I'm not sure if Pastor Williams knows Onie Jones, but their stories are similar. Onie is a woman who once lived in a wealthy suburb of Memphis called Germantown. The problem facing Onie was that she read the story of Jesus and it wouldn't let her go. She sold her home and moved to a blighted community in the heart of Memphis known as Binghampton. As a white female, statistics would say that she was out of place. But Onie believed that all people had a commonality—they had been created in the image of God.

Upon arriving in her new community, she took seriously the spiritual discipline of hospitality and intentionally engaged in a ministry of presence. The front entrance of her home was a revolving door for neighbors who came in and out of Onie's to eat at a community table and to engage in Bible studies focused on covenant love and peace-making. With a courageous passion to see people unite, Onie enabled a paradigm shift in the neighborhood.

A few blocks from Onie's home, a Masonic lodge became vacant, and Onie wrote a few friends inquiring about their willingness to invest in a vision to remodel the lodge into a community center, coffee shop, and cultural arts center. Onie's vision was to "break down walls of hostility between races, rich and poor, and provide a positive street-corner alternative for neighborhood children." Since December of 2006, Caritas Village has functioned as a community hub.

Onie and Pastor Williams are two examples of fearlessness that engages suffering, and this engagement ultimately links us with the greater suffering of the world. The suffering bystander becomes the suffering participant, because that's what it means to be fully human.

Unintentional Suffering Outside of Our Control

Many people suffer as innocent victims. These are the people who have been initiated into clubs they never signed up for. No one wants to become a member of clubs called Widowed, Miscarried, Sexually Abused by Stepdad,

Cancer-Stricken, Taken Advantage Of, Cheated On, or Bankrupted.

Memphis is home to St. Jude Children's Research Hospital. Walk down one hallway, and you'll see reminders that this world isn't right. Kayci and I have visited St. Jude on a few occasions. Our first visit was because we had some friends from Abilene, Texas, whose seven-year-old was fighting leukemia. We followed the instructions and took the elevator to the second floor. As we rounded the corner to the waiting room we saw a small child with no hair who was attempting to hug his grandfather through the protective glass window. There's not an author alive who could structure words to describe the emotions of that moment. It will drop you to your knees to thank God for the high temperature and runny nose that hits your child a couple of times a year.

The first form of suffering—Intentional Suffering Because We Make Poor Decisions—makes sense. We don't like it. We don't want to suffer this way. But we know that people have the ability and power to cause great harm.

The second form of suffering—Intentional Suffering Because We Decide to Enter into Brokenness—is what good stories are made of. This is the courage that heals a broken a world.

The third form—Unintentional Suffering Outside of Our

Control—is what rattles us to the core. It is one of the primary reasons I felt compelled to write this book. Scripture doesn't provide answers to all of the questions that come from this form of suffering. This is where many pastors and authors lose credibility with me, because they feel as if they must have an answer to every question. They're unable to embrace the mystery of God. And when they launch into theological explanations, they tend to babble like pagans. Sometimes, suffering is permission to wrestle with questions that lead to maturity and growth, not answers.

This book doesn't spend much time on suffering from poor decision making. That discussion needs to take place, and others have done a wonderful job engaging in this conversation on a broad scale. I feel compelled to spend time wrestling with the other two forms of suffering, because they often go hand in hand. One informs the other. Since it is true that we will all suffer, it is also true that how we suffer will greatly impact how we live and engage the world around us.

When Jenny became sick, we had just made a decision to sell our suburban home and to join the neighborhood Onie had moved into. Three weeks before Jenny entered the hospital, we attended an event in a Memphis community known as Binghampton. Shane Claiborne—an author, activist, and intentional neighbor in his Philadelphia neighborhood—was visiting Binghampton. Kayci and I had been wrestling for months about the decision of doing something different with our lives, and this night would provide us with the inspiration to move forward on our adventure. With his East Tennessee accent, Shane spoke about Jesus' radical commitment to enter into pain and oppression so that he could redeem the mind, body, and soul. Most everyone attending the event had read *The Irresistible Revolution*, but it was the question-and-answer session that allowed us to process some of the values and principles discussed in his book.

Kayci, holding our four-month-old child and standing in the far back corner, raised her hand for one of the final questions.

"Shane, hi. I'm Kayci, and I love so much of what you shared tonight. But I have a family. I have two little boys. How do you do this with a family? My questions are about schools and safety. What would you say to a mother like me?"

His response went something like this: "Well, I'm not the one to be answering this question because I don't have children. There's not a neighborhood in existence where you can guarantee the safety of your children. Of course, you have to be responsible, but what you need to decide is this: Does the beauty of raising children in diversity outweigh the fear of what might happen? As for education, we have families in our initiative who send their children to the neighborhood school, others who have chosen the private school route, and still others who homeschool.

What they have all found is that they raise their children with values of simplicity and diversity that can't be taught elsewhere."

So, Shane didn't provide a concrete answer for either of Kayci's questions, but his response provided a framework for us to make a decision that would alter our future.

Within a three-week period in early 2010, we made a family decision to enter into an impoverished neighborhood to live among others, and we also found ourselves in deep grief due to the sickness and death of Jenny.

In some crazy way, Jenny's death empowered a deeper passion for us to engage the world with intentionality. We are in Memphis now because we couldn't pass up the beauty of the culture and we couldn't pass up the beauty of the struggle. In many ways, Memphis has saved me. I'm not talking about being saved from hell into heaven. It has saved me from pride, selfishness, escapism, and materialism. It has converted me, like Peter's conversion in Acts 10. He knew Jesus. He had been used by God to save the souls of thousands, but in Acts 10 he had an experience that converted him to the greater mission of Jesus that must spread to non-Jews. I needed a new conversion that would lead me to deeper places with God.

Memphis did this by teaching me how to suffer well.

7

IS MEMPHIS IN TEXAS?

You see, I'll be one of those people who live to be history makers at a young age. Oh, I'll have moments, good and bad, but I will wipe away the bad and only remember the good. In fact that's all I remember, just good moments, nothing in between, just living my life to the fullest. I'll be one of those people who go somewhere with a mission, an awesome plan, a world-changing plan, and nothing will hold me back. I'll set an example for others, I will pray for direction.

—FRANCIS CHAN QUOTING BROOKE BRONKOWSKI[1]

Grief will change the way you interpret the past, and it will give you a new lens to view the future. I was first opened up to the greater suffering in the world when I took a one-week trip to San Francisco my freshman year of college. We stayed in a halfway house, living with ex-cons, murderers, and drug dealers. That one week altered my life and transformed my faith. I discovered that homeless people have names. They have stories. I also began to see that God is passionate about the injustices in our world. Suffering became real, because suffering involves people— real people. At the time, I was uncertain where this new epiphany would lead me.

Years ago, many people came to Jesus asking to *see* so they could *believe.* I do this. If you told me there was a three-legged man in a circus who could swallow swords, I would want to see it (either live or on YouTube) before I believe it.

Maybe the reason faith is called *faith* is because seeing doesn't lead to belief, but belief transforms the way we see. This lesson is vital to our maturity in life.

When Jenny became sick, I was immersed in my ministry in Memphis. Scars had become contagious. When you choose to associate with the downtrodden and broken-hearted, you begin to carry their pain with you. You can't shake the images burned into your memory from walking into depleted homes, encountering starving children, and seeing the vicious cycles of drug use and drug dealing.

While many people questioned our move to Memphis, Jenny endorsed it from the beginning. She knew that life is about adventure and journey. She understood that the way of Jesus is to run into the fight, not from the fight. I don't want God to visit me one day and say, "Why do you keep playing it safe?"

▪   ▪   ▪

Hope House is a day-care center in Memphis serving children ages six months to five years who have been affected by the AIDS epidemic. Ninety percent of the kids come from families who make less than $10,000 per year. Nearly one-third of the children are known to be HIV positive, and all of them have at least one parent who is infected. Hope House opened in 1995, and they are currently the only facility in the state of Tennessee designed to meet the unique demands of children directly affected by this disease.

What do you call a place like this? The Bible calls it a place where Jesus tends to show up.

I walked into Hope House one day with another pastor in town. More than a dozen kids sat on the floor of a classroom as a worship minister led them in some silly children's songs. I decided to sit down with the kids, but before I made it to the carpet, the kids were all over me. They were climbing on my shoulders, and they couldn't resist touching my ears, eyes, and hair. For a guy who's half germaphobe, I had a moment when I envisioned Howie Mandel next to me wishing he had the power to click his heels and disappear.

One kid, probably three years old, sat in my lap and just stared at me.

I leaned over during a song and whispered into his ear, "What's your name, buddy?"

He said, "My name is Tyrone."

I said, "Good to meet you, Tyrone. Do you know what my name is?"

Silence. He just continued to stare.

I whispered, "You can call me Mr. Josh."

He shook his head and said, "No. I want to call you my daddy."

I entered into Hope House thinking I was going to hang out with some poor sick kids. I left encountering Jesus in the eyes of a little kid named Tyrone. I drove home with tears in my eyes as I called my wife and said, "Baby, we need to think about adopting some kids."

Memphis has shaped the way I think of Jesus. Or maybe Jesus has shaped the way I think of Memphis.

I began praying a prayer when I arrived in Memphis. It was a prayer that would rock my world. I asked God to lead me through the streets of Memphis and to open my eyes to see the city with new perspective. With the words of others who have gone before me, I began praying for my heart to be broken by the things that break the heart of God. He began leading me on a journey that would wreck my life, because it would pull me outside of the confines of my suburban bubble.

The first twenty-seven years of my life were spent in Texas. In the spring of 2008, Kayci and I felt the call of God to Memphis, Tennessee. I don't know what other way to name it but *calling.* The word *calling* wasn't a word we used in my religious upbringing, and when it was used, it seemed that people were being called to places where they made more money and had more luxuries. I was never really sure how that lined up with the words and life of Jesus. Others would use the word as if God was speaking a call into their lives every single day, when Scripture seems to depict God calling people every few decades.

We felt *called* to Memphis, and it was then we discovered something about our fellow Texans—they have egos. Before we left, people would place their hands on our shoulders, shake their heads, and say, "Bless you, my child." It was like we were going to the moon. People blessed us and mourned for us, like we were becoming aliens and strangers in a foreign land.

After arriving in Memphis, members of Sycamore View Church would approach me after sermons, lean in, and whisper, "We're one of you."

My response: "What do you mean?"

"We're from the Lone Star State"

"Okay," and then I would think to myself, *I'm from the land of egocentric maniacs who've been drinking the Texas-Is-Better Kool-Aid.*

Kayci and I were expecting our second child in August of 2009, and Texans offered to send us Texas dirt to spread on the floor of the delivery room just so our child could be born on Texas soil. People from Michigan and Idaho don't do these kinds of things, do they?

I knew a Christian tattoo artist in Abilene who had a license to tattoo people in four different states, but he told me that only in Texas would people come in wanting the Texas flag or the outline of the state on their bicep or shoulder blade. People from Delaware and Rhode Island don't do these things. I don't think Dover pride is that deep.

But the number one response we received from people when they heard we were moving to Memphis was this: "Have you *been* to Memphis? Have you *heard* about that place?"

Some would say that I have chosen to minister in a city full of impossibilities.

We were drawn to Memphis because we desire to do ministry and raise a family in the midst of racial tension, in a place with a large disparity between the rich and the poor. You can find that anywhere, but it is intensified in my city. We desired to see what God is up to in a place many people have written off as corrupt, lost, and impossible.

When I look around Memphis, I see so much to appreciate. Memphis is a city with a rich history of culture and food. We're known for our pork barbecue and for being the place of the Kings: Elvis the King, B. B. King, and Dr. King. There's so much about Memphis to love—from FedEx to soul food, AutoZone to basketball, from Sun Studio to the birthplace of the blues.

But Memphis also has a reputation for violence, crime, racism, and division. A few years ago *Forbes* magazine listed us as the second most miserable city in the United States to live in. For years we've been either at the top or near the top of the charts recording violent crime. Our city is often portrayed on the hit TV show *The First 48*. And who can ignore the historical meaning behind Auction Street near downtown.

But Kayci and I believed that this city had a lot to teach us about life.

Maybe it's my calling—maybe I've seen it and I can't go back—but I want to witness impossibilities as they bow down to the name of Jesus. I do what I do because I believe in the power of the Resurrection, and I'm convinced that the same power that was at work in lifting Jesus from the grave is at work in this world today to bring the dead to life.

There are nights when I turn on the news and hear of another homicide or child abduction, and I'm tempted to join in the pessimism that says, "Some cities are helpless." But my commitment to Jesus won't let me go there.

I want to be able to read the newspaper, see corruption, and then push the paper aside as if to say, "The chaos and unrest in this world are not my problems. They are not my issues." But my baptism—the fact that I died and rose with Christ—won't let me, because my baptism tells me that I am caught up (I'm a participant) in the rhythm of creation. I've been ushered into a new way of living. My eyes have been opened to see that, like it or not, I'm linked with all of humanity. It is my personal restoration that commissions me to see that others are redeemable as well.

I have days when I just want to live life in comfortable places. But the problem is that I take Communion on Sundays. And when I eat the bread and drink the cup, it's not just a moment to remember the sacrifice of Jesus; it's a formative moment that begs for these same hands to serve in a way that will create life in and for others, not to retreat from it.

Recently, a story was released about a high school in Memphis that reported over ninety pregnancies in the 2010–2011 school year. Not only did it make national news, it found its way into a script for the hit show *Glee*. You know you have made the news when *Glee* decides to talk about you. Letterman and Leno are one thing; making it onto *Glee* is another. In the show, substitute teacher Holly Holliday, played by guest star Gwyneth Paltrow, says, "I just read in the newspaper that ninety high school girls in a Memphis school district got pregnant within three months. I mean, it is Tennessee, but still we got to shake things up. Information is power."

I thought to myself, *Wow! Memphis leads the U.S. in infant mortality rates. We have more children who die before the age of one than some third-world countries. And, we have ninety pregnant girls in one high school at the same time. Something isn't right.*

And you know what, something *isn't* right.

Something isn't right with fifteen-year-olds walking into math class in their third trimesters. But something also isn't right when you have people living in the same city claiming to follow Jesus who mute the local news so that their spouse can hear them call the girls "sluts" and "whores."

The easiest thing to do is to escape. But despite the flight to the suburbs that has taken place in our cities and in our churches, the Bible doesn't teach escapism as the answer to the world. Jesus didn't teach people to flee blight and depressed living conditions. He taught a different way. He taught that the God-honoring way to live is as people who create life for others instead of controlling life for themselves. He taught that it's not just about how to rid yourself of sin but how you live and interact with your neighbors. So, if I choose to refrain from R-rated movies, trashy music, and porn but don't know my neighbor, I am still not living as one who is aligned with the values of God.

Our covenant with Jesus is to see the scars of the world as opportunities for restoration, deliverance, and reconciliation. And when we give in to pessimistic portrayals of the world around us, as if the world were irretrievably lost, we are no longer being true to the power of our baptisms, which are rooted in the resurrection of Jesus.

God's way is along the path of intrusion and involvement.

God's way is a path of descending into the depths of pain and raw expressions of reality.

Maybe this is why the adventure of following Jesus becomes a life-altering course.

And maybe this is why it's often a path unchosen.

8

LIVED EXPERIENCES

I wonder, then, if when people say life is meaningless, what they really mean is their lives are meaningless. I wonder if they've chosen to believe their whole existence is unremarkable, and are projecting their dreary life on the rest of us.

. . . People who live good stories are too busy to write about them. Nobody ever strapped a typewriter to the back of an elephant and wrote a novel while hunting wild game.

. . . My life was a blank page, and all I was putting on the page were words. I didn't want to live in words anymore; I wanted to live in sweat and pain.

—DONALD MILLER[1]

I learned early on in my ministry in Memphis that the word *racism* is a trigger word.

Many of my white friends are eager to forget the past. They want people to get over it. I just never hear that from my black friends. Maybe it's because when you have been a part of the race that has benefited from the system, you haven't been pressed down by the injustice, so it's a lot easier to suggest that everyone should just forget the past. The greater challenge is learning to remember in healthy ways.

In one sermon, I alluded to the fact that prior to Saul's conversion in Acts 9, he was a racist and would have fit in well in some Southern cities. I admit, it probably could have been said differently. One woman took offense and handed a written note to an elder. He approached me about the subject. That's how it usually works in my tribe. If you're ticked at a minister, you go to the elders and expect them to fix it. I called the woman that afternoon to discuss the comment I had made, and she said, "Josh, wait until you've experienced some sh** in life before you say some of the things you say."

I couldn't get that out of my mind. It stuck with me. Sometimes when criticism comes I struggle to shake it. It's kind of like Memphis barbecue; it usually takes seventy-two hours to get it out of my system. It wasn't the context of the woman's statement that kept me up at night. It was the sheer reality that her statement was true; nothing transforms a person like lived experiences.

You can preach all you want about loving the poor, but if your life isn't leading you into deeper relationships with the poor, why would anyone be inspired by your words?

The best sermons aren't born from commentaries or scholarly work but from lives lived and lessons learned from real experiences.

■   ■   ■

In his book *The Word on the Street*, Charles L. Campbell discusses the difference between physical location and social location. Both of these have a huge impact on the way you interpret Scripture.

For example, "social location" means this: I'm a white, middle-class American with a master's degree from a private Christian university, and I was raised in a healthy two-parent home. All of these attributes have an impact on my interpretation of Scripture. At one time, it was easy for me to downplay statements by Jesus like "Blessed are you who are poor" or "sell your possessions and give to the poor." I would spiritualize these verses—meaning that I would make them about the heart, therefore stripping them of any literal interpretations—*because they were outside of my social experiences.* My culture raised me to put clauses on Jesus' words.

But "physical location" forces us outside of our preferred experiences by asking different questions: What if we took a group of people to study the Sermon on the Mount at the food court in a shopping mall? How would Jesus' words about not worrying about clothes, food, and what to drink come to life in an environment of consumption? What if churches attempted to study the stories of Jesus touching sick people and lepers at AIDS clinics or homeless shelters?

Most people who read the Bible read it while sitting in

safe places: either within their homes or within the walls of a church building. There's nothing wrong with this. God enlightens the heart and mind because of such devotion. But Jesus rarely taught his disciples while standing on religious space. Jesus taught on busy roads, by lakes while fishermen took their lunch breaks, on hillsides, and in pagan-filled cities like Caesarea Philippi. Jesus invited followers on an adventure, and he took advantage of the journey by telling stories that stimulated our imagination to think bigger about this created life.

Maybe Jesus still aspires to teach in such ways.

In the movie *Remember the Titans,* Coach Boone, played by Denzel Washington, found himself coaching a team that was racially divided. Their capacity to hate was deeply embedded in their culture, and it had seeped into the corners of their hearts. Coach Boone, like many football coaches today, realized that high school football is more than *X*s and *O*s; it's about developing character.

Early one morning at preseason camp, Coach Boone sets off the bullhorn, awakening the players long before the sun begins to rise. The team, along with the assistant coaches, gather outside, and Coach Boone leads them on a jog. He is the only one who knows where they are going. This isn't a fitness exercise to increase stamina. There is a lesson to be taught, and the location is significant.

They finally come to a stop, and the players bend over, trying to catch their breaths. They look at their head coach; he is glancing out into a field.

This is where they fought the battle of Gettysburg. Fifty thousand men died right here on this field, fighting the same fight that we are still fighting among ourselves today. . . . You listen, and you take a lesson from the dead. If we don't come together right now on this hallowed ground, we too will be destroyed, just like they were.

Coach Boone could have said his piece in the cafeteria at their camp, or even on the football field, but there are some words, some lessons, that resonate with greater power in the right location. Coach Boone chose Gettysburg to teach his team about coming together as one. And his words performed. The team was changed.

Jesus was a brilliant teacher. He knew that there were times when location mattered. In Matthew 15, religious leaders challenged Jesus on traditions. He proceeded to instruct the crowds around him concerning God's definition of what is clean and unclean. It had nothing to do with washing your hands before you eat. It had everything to do with the condition of your heart. The story that immediately follows begins, "Leaving that place, Jesus withdrew to the region of Tyre and Sidon."[2]

This wasn't a neighboring city. Tyre and Sidon were on the way to nowhere. To make matters worse, it was a region populated with pagans, Gentiles, and unclean people. Do you see what Jesus was doing? He led his disciples to a place with unclean people, so that he could teach them a lesson about who is clean and who is unclean, who is in and who is out.

He did the same thing in Matthew 16. Again, Jesus was approached by agitators. This time they wanted a sign. After a few words of rebuke, Jesus instructed his disciples about the yeast of the Pharisees, which was hypocrisy and void of life.

Then, we read this, "When Jesus came to the region of Caesarea Philippi . . ."[3]

Caesarea Philippi was located twenty-five miles from the religious communities of Galilee. It was a region known for pagan worship, shrines, and temples to the god Pan. To awake and entice their god, the people of the city would engage in horrible deeds. Jesus led the disciples to a place their parents had warned them never to enter. As they neared the city gates, they probably had the same feeling teenagers have today when they have told their parents they are going to Chili's but their friends pull them into the parking lot at Hooters.

Of all places for Jesus to ask about his identity, it was

in Caesarea Philippi. A city whose walls had windows and crevices holding shrines of pagan gods. This is where Jesus asks, "Who do people say the Son of Man is? . . . Who do you say I am?"[4] Of all places for Jesus to declare that his church was going to be built upon a rock—Caesarea Philippi. Jesus led them to a city full of darkness to make a statement about his power and mission.

Memphis has taught me that when prayer gets beyond whining about knee joints and three-day-old coughs and into the arena of praying in accordance with God's reigning kingdom, our experiences begin to reflect the life of someone on a journey. God began peeling off layers of religious upbringing, so that he could show me the power of transformed eyes. After all, God's been performing surgery on eyes for thousands of years. Two of his most notable patients are guys you've probably heard of before: Moses and Saul.

Moses was born as a Hebrew into oppression, but he was raised as an Egyptian with power. Something happened in Exodus 2:11 that changed Moses's course: "He went out to where his own people were and saw them at their hard labor. He *saw* an Egyptian beating a Hebrew, one of his own people."

Unless Moses had been locked up in the palace for the early part of his life, he had seen this forced labor before. Only blindness could have accounted for a complete unawareness of the oppressed Hebrew people. For years, Moses must have seen the oppression and ignored it. It just didn't have an effect on him.

But that day, Moses went out to his people, and he "saw" their forced labor.

In Hebrew, this is the word *ra'ah*. (Say it a few times just for fun.)

This is more than just seeing an object in front of you. This indicates a deep emotional involvement.

Ra'ah describes what God did after each day of creating in Genesis 1: "God *saw* what he had made and it was good." You've probably seen pictures of a figure with his arm stretched out, and in his palm is a globe. It makes for a pretty cool picture but a lousy portrayal of God the Creator. When God saw what he had made, there was an emotional attachment. God didn't look upon his creation as a faraway figure glancing through a telescope. Instead, God was overcome with a deep sense of involvement. God stepped into his creation. Now that's an image worth savoring.

So, for Moses, this meant that now, after forty years of seeing the oppression, this one day, somehow, a form of sympathy entered into him. This suffering overwhelmed him to where it became his own. Moses resonated with the oppressed, and he felt compelled to act.

Moses's experience with *ra'ah* is a pivotal component

in the deliverance of God's people from Egypt. Moses *sees* differently, and his life changes.

Could it be that God not only wants people to have a *heart* for the world, but he also wants us to have *eyes* for the world? Maybe God's desire is for his people to develop a sense of *ra'ah*. After all, we have been made in his image.

Fast-forward maybe two thousand years, and you come to the story of Saul.

In Acts 9:1–2, we read, "Meanwhile, Saul was still breathing out murderous threats against the Lord's disciples. He went to the high priest and asked him for letters to the synagogues in Damascus, so that if he found any who belonged to the Way, whether men or women, he might take them as prisoners to Jerusalem."

He was on the road to Damascus.

The mission—or, as some would say, the strategery— was to arrest the followers of the Way.

The overall plan: fill the prisons and jails of Jerusalem with these followers, because if they could confine these Jesus lovers in one location, then they could keep this message from spreading like a contagious virus.

Saul led people into Damascus with a hit list. They had names, faces, and addresses. It was as if they had printed off Google maps and knew the exact locations of the synagogues and possible escape routes. They had one mission: to arrest these people and transport them to Jerusalem.

Maybe you've heard the story before: a bright light forced Saul to the ground, which was followed by a brief yet powerful conversation between Jesus and the Jesus hater (4–6).

JESUS: "Saul, Saul, why do you persecute me?"
SAUL: "Who are you, Lord?"
JESUS: "I am Jesus, whom you are persecuting. Now get up and enter the city, and you will be told what you must do."

Here's what's interesting: this experience left Saul temporarily blind. The one who was leading other soldiers into a city was now the one being led. Grisham, Sparks, nor Lucado could have written a better plot.

The next three days had to have gone by at a horse-and-buggy pace. No food. No water. No sight.

On day three, Ananias and Saul ended up in the same room. Saul probably knew the name—Ananias may have been number fourteen on the hit list. They skipped over the meet-and-greet session and got straight to business. Ananias laid his hands on Saul, spoke a word of God into his life, and we read, "*something like scales* fell from Saul's eyes, and he could see again (18)."

Why did God go for the eyes?

"Something like scales" had to fall from Saul's eyes during this conversion, because Saul had tainted vision. The world "Saul saw" (pardon the tongue twister) was a black-and-white world. Either you're in or you're out. Either you're a Jew or you're a Gentile. Either you're a clapper or you're a nonclapper. Either you're traditional or you're progressive. Either you're a Democrat or you're a Republican. Either you're a Red Sox fan (which means you might get into heaven) or you're a Yankees fan (which means you have no shot).

In order for God to convert Saul into Paul in a way that would take this good news to the ends of the earth, God had to change the way Saul *saw* the world.

This was the first ever LASIK surgery.

God went for the eyes. He could have gone for the ears or even straight to the heart, but he went for the eyes.

Paul would forever look back on this day as the day that he encountered Jesus, but even more so, it was the day that he learned to see the world through the eyes of Jesus.

So, I began praying for God to help me *really* see the world. This began an adventure that would unpack hidden passions in my life. It enabled me to sniff out the presence of God in places saturated with suffering and pain.

What would a Friday night with an undercover cop, a

ride-along with a Memphis firefighter, intentional drives to unknown parts of the city, and a meaningful relationship with a two-year-old victim of the AIDS epidemic who can curse like a sailor do to one's motivations and priorities?

I would soon find out. Jesus was inviting me into a scar-filled world. My unmarked body would soon join in the mission.

9

CURSING TODDLERS

I find that Holy Week is draining; no matter how many times I have lived through his crucifixion, my anxiety about his resurrection is undiminished—I am terrified that, this year, it won't happen; that, that year, it didn't. Anyone can be sentimental about the Nativity; any fool can feel like a Christian at Christmas. But Easter is the main event; if you don't believe in the resurrection, you're not a believer.

—JOHN IRVING [1]

Maybe grief is meant to form us into compassionate people who care about all forms of suffering and the injustices taking place all around us. This passion to step into oppressed situations quickly became a reality that launched me into an adventure of restoration possibilities.

The more time I spent with Jesus, the more I felt him inviting me out of my office and into the streets of Memphis in order to broaden my capacity to love. This journey led me to a friend who has been a firefighter for more than twenty-five years. He was kind enough to orchestrate a ride-along with a fire chief on a Friday night. The challenge would be to experience life outside of my bubble and to walk away still believing that the resurrection of Jesus is the best news for the world.

We arrived at the fire station around 3:30 p.m., and our first call came thirty minutes later. With sirens blasting, we sped down streets and arrived at a small one-bedroom home in an impoverished neighborhood to find a large, elderly woman lying on the ground. She had fallen that morning at 7:00 a.m., and it took her nine hours to crawl across her twelve-by-twelve-foot bedroom to reach a phone and call 911. This was the beginning of a night when I saw very clearly how all of creation groans for adoption and redemption.

Within the hour, we were called onto two different scenes where pedestrians had been hit by cars. After arriving, I stood in the middle of a four-lane road surrounded by police cars, fire trucks, and ambulances. The lights seemed like disco lights at a skating rink, but this was nothing like being with friends about to do the limbo or the hokey-pokey. This was a moment when relatives received phone calls that altered lives.

As the ambulance drove off with soon-to-be hospital patients, I stood there with firefighters and cops thinking that we might take a few minutes to debrief. After all, that's what pastors do in these moments. We are inclined to sit around asking questions about how the experience made us feel and how we saw God in the moment and what we could do to make it safer for people to cross the road. My firefighter friends took a different approach. This was just another day on the job for them. They knew that if they allowed themselves to be drawn into the suffering of all those they serve it would only take days before the joy of life was sucked from them. So, they looked at each other, decided they were hungry, and then one guy spotted an Interstate Barbecue joint down the street. One moment we were standing over a broken body, and the next moment we were ordering barbecue nachos.

Firefighters are fascinating people. They are men and women of courage whose job is to enter places full of pain with the expectation and expertise to rescue and relieve. Firefighters don't enter homes to sip tea with strangers while watching *American Idol*. They are called into the scenes of trauma and chaos. It's no wonder some firefighters seem detached from their encounters and pessimistic about possible restoration. Being called into the misery of life can do this to you.

We were finishing our meal when we received a call that an eleven-year-old kid had attempted suicide. I grabbed the last few nachos on my plate as we ran out of the restaurant to a scene that would forever be etched into my mind. We pulled into an apartment complex, and dozens of cops were already on the scene. The kid had come home from school and, for a reason, tied a belt around his neck like a noose, hung the other end on a doorknob, and kicked his feet out from underneath him in an attempt to strangle himself. When we arrived on the scene, the paramedics had already resuscitated him. My friend ushered me past all of the other police officers and put me on the ambulance. Staring down at an eleven-year-old who had tried to take his own life, I tried to make sense of what I believe about the power of the resurrection. My prayers weren't for God to make things right one day at the end of time. I wanted the power of God that raised Jesus from the dead to break into that ambulance right then, to break into that twelve-by-twelve-foot bedroom, to break onto the streets of Memphis and alleviate the suffering in the lives of real people.

There's oppression and bondage all around me. I've seen it out car windows driving through some of the most crime-ridden neighborhoods. I've seen it with a friend who is an undercover cop in car washes where people cut up crack right in front of me. I've seen it in some of the nicest neighborhoods in this city as I watched men waxing their new Mercedes, knowing that if they spent the same amount of time investing in their marriages and hanging out with their kids that their relationships might be different.

I'm often judgmental about the white flight that took place in the sixties and seventies, but I attempt to keep it in perspective. I want to be a man of grace. People moved farther out, but churches also abandoned their calling and mission field to cater to neighborhoods with water fountains and newer shopping malls. But for most who moved away from inner-city life, it wasn't intentional to abandon or reject the mission of Jesus. Many were good people. There was an element of wanting to escape the crime and violence, but there was also the desire to escape the pain and suffering. The suburbs provided street corners that weren't full of signs of the homeless or crowded bus stops. People didn't have to watch six-year-olds walking to school with decade-old hand-me-downs. All of the construction represented progress and new life.

But here's where we all have to be careful. When we become selective in our understanding of the world—because quite honestly, it can be easier to hold up a pro-life picket sign than to foster relationships with people who are struggling with the decision to keep or abort—we have an inconsistent ethic of life. It becomes difficult to care about people from the womb to the tomb. There is danger when we parent in a way that shields our children from any form of poverty that seems to be a threat, yet we have no qualms about walking our children through shopping malls, running up credit card bills on the latest gadgets and the shoes we might wear twice in a year.

Becoming selective moralists can easily become one of the greatest threats to Christ being formed in us.

If we aren't careful, our moral convictions will simply become methods to stiff-arm the suffering of the world, in the very places Jesus seemed to step into.

Imagine a world in which Christians make it a point to live not in the same neighborhoods as their closest friends, but on different streets in every neighborhood in their communities. What if Christians made the simple commitment to be good neighbors? This kind of intentionality is the invitation from a God who resides with the rich *and* the poor.

Nehemiah is a book about the revival of Jerusalem, and it's a story that spoke deeply into our desire to move into Memphis. You see, as Nehemiah begins, the people of Israel have returned from exile, and there is a city to be built. A revived city was essential to the revival of the people. They needed a place to call home. A place with walls, fountains, and a temple.

After the city was rebuilt there was a problem. People still lived in towns outside of the Jerusalem city limits. In Nehemiah 11, "the leaders of the people settled in Jerusalem. The rest of the people cast lots to bring one out of every ten of them to live in Jerusalem, the holy city, while the remaining nine were to stay in their own towns. The people commended all who volunteered to live in Jerusalem."

They needed people living in the city in order to ignite true revival. The request wasn't for the entire community living on the outskirts to put their homes on the market. The request was simply for 10 percent to take a risk and to be a part of a different story.

When I was in seminary, I had a professor who told us that roughly one hundred million people in America—that is one-third of America's population—live in apartment complexes. Out of the one hundred million, only 1 percent are affiliated with a church. This should reveal something about a primary mission field around us. As this professor travels to consult with churches, he often asks church leadership how many of them live in apartment complexes. The number of elders and ministers who have chosen to reside in one of the primary mission fields in our nation is slim to none. What do we do with something like this?

I understand that some of you reading this book are currently living in small towns where everyone knows one another. I'm writing out of a context where there is a great divide between suburban life and city life. It is evident in everything from politics to education, to the "us" and "them" used to verbalize the distinction between the two. With that said, there are many people who are committed to unity, and some of the efforts that are being made in our cities to destroy existing strongholds are thriving . . . and it gives me hope.

■   ■   ■

When I began writing this book, Kayci and I lived in the suburbs of Memphis. When we chose to move here, no one encouraged us live within the city limits—and I mean no one. We purchased a home, and we thrived in our neighborhood, loving neighbors and enjoying the quiet. But there was this constant nagging that kept me up at night.

We sold our home in the summer of 2011 and moved into an "at-risk,"[2] or "swing,"[3] neighborhood in the city. We wanted to make sure that our move came from a healthy place. We didn't want to go suffering from a Messianic complex, moving into a rough area to be the savior of the neighborhood. On numerous occasions, God reminded us that he has already taken up residence in the communities many have deemed as lost or "not okay to drive through." We just wanted to join him there. For us, it boiled down to this: we felt like we needed to be in the 10 percent described in Nehemiah 11:1–2. We wanted to be in the middle of God's desire to reconcile the world to himself. We wanted to raise our family in the midst of diversity. And lastly, we didn't want to have to make appointments just to be with people outside of our primary social experiences; we wanted to be among them.

It took twelve months to sell our home. Needless to say, it wasn't the best time (economically speaking) to sell a home, and during the long wait we received our fair share of criticism:

- "You know we won't be able to drive our car to visit you anymore. We'll have to fly, because we can't leave our car parked outside of your home. Something might happen to it."
- "Have you watched *The First 48* recently?"
- "I think you're too idealistic."
- I think my favorite is this one: "Have you thought about the kids?"

Close friends attempted to offer advice but, in actuality, they became like Job's friends. Some told us that because our home didn't sell immediately it was a sign that God didn't want us to move. For us, it was simply a sign that it was a tough housing market.

This isn't about becoming heroes who will have our story retold. It's about being faithful to a calling in our lives. We've heard gunshots at night, but we've also experienced love and relationships in ways that can't be experienced anywhere else.

Discipleship continually invites Christ followers to join Jesus on a journey, a journey in which scars are inevitable. In fact, they often become marks of transformation. It takes some guts for biblical writers to say some of the things they say. Paul sounds like he's nuts when he says stuff like "I want to know Christ—yes, to know the power of his resurrection and participation in his sufferings, becoming like him in his death."[4]

Participation in his sufferings?

Becoming like him in his death?

Who says this kind of stuff? Who makes these kinds of claims? I guess those who make such claims actually believe that suffering and death are part of a bigger story, part of a better story.

My good friend Pam Cope lost her son, Jantsen, when he was fifteen years old. He came home from football practice one day, took a nap, and never woke up. Soon after Jantsen had been conceived, Pam had been devastated to find out she would be unable to have her firstborn child naturally. They had to cut her open. A C-section was the only way. She remembered expressing frustration to God at the time, because she was aware of the health risks. And then there was a scar that would be there for life.

Today, she is constantly aware of that scar. It doesn't go away. Every time she steps into the shower she is reminded that she didn't have a natural birth, but it's more than that now. It's a reminder that Jantsen was born into this world and is now gone.

Maybe scars are a gift. They remind us that we are living life. And isn't this what God wants? For us to live life. For us to be present in the here and now?

Some people choose to cross their fingers hoping that they'll get into heaven in the end. Maybe this was the motivation of the rich young ruler who approached Jesus. After all, his question was about eternal life.

"What good thing must I do to have eternal life?"[5]

In other words, the guy was making sure that he had done enough to qualify. Had he said the right prayer? Been baptized? Believed something in his heart? Tithed consistently?

Don't miss the intentionality in Jesus' response: "If you want to enter into life . . ."[6]

The young rich guy asked about eternal life, and Jesus responded by inviting him into real life. It's not that Jesus doesn't talk about heaven and hell; it's just that he doesn't talk about it as much as some people think he does. Jesus' primary concern is that people live on purpose. This has always been God's intent.

Jesus lived in a way that quickly garnered him a reputation as a friend of sinners. How can followers of Jesus regain this reputation today? How can churches become "friends of sinners" and not just exclusive social clubs with flashy slogans or billboard ads?

One of my greatest fears in life is to be a living contradiction. It's the fear of not living a life that aligns itself with radical sermons about Jesus. It's a fear of modeling good citizenship for my boys while failing to model faithful risk taking.

I was with a mentor recently who cried when he told several other young ministers that he used to go into a depression every Sunday night because the sermons he preached about the radical nature of Jesus on Sunday mornings didn't line up with the life he was living the rest of the week.

Taking Jesus seriously is bound to bring physical, emotional, and social scars. And do we really believe that God enters into the scars of life?

Maybe to redeem the scars.

Maybe just to be present in the scar-filled moments.

My prayer of learning to love the people of Memphis led me back to Hope House. This time, I was back to get involved. They have a buddy system that they've struggled to get up and running. Basically, they are eager to find men and women who will devote one hour a week to one of their students. Without knowing what I was getting into, I signed up.

They partnered me with a kid who was in need of a mentor. He was two years old, and the staff warned me that he liked to hit and curse. I thought they were referring to words like "stupid" or "shut up." Those were the types of words that got me in trouble as a kid. After one day with my buddy, Matthew, I realized the warning was for real. This kid knew how to say words that I didn't know existed until I was in fourth or fifth grade. Words like "shit" and "bitch" simply flowed out of his limited two-year-old vocabulary. This should tell you something about his environment. But somehow, through the grace of God, we formed a connection. Little did I know that this buddy who had been placed in my life was being used by God to teach me about life.

Six months before Jenny died, she had a dream to bring Kidstand—a traveling ministry to reach kids for Jesus—to Memphis. Sometimes I envision Jenny, healed and made whole, dancing on the streets of Memphis with the kids who have died of AIDS and lack of prenatal care. Jenny would adore Matthew.

Maybe the reason I connected with Matthew so quickly is because the scars I see in him are the same scars I find in myself. We are two people who bear the scars of a world gone berserk. Yet, we are also two people who bear the scars of a world thick with God's presence.

PART 3

SCARRED COMMUNITIES

Death: His Sting and Defeat
And I saw him: Death, with his mighty sting,
Exhaling in every breath the plight he brings
To the grave he gave victory
Triumphing over life with the fear of endless sleep
Endlessly we hide from our mortality

We are all dying, there's no other way
I see him in Haitian and Japanese earthquakes
He's Hating the Escapees of his cruel wakes
I see him in poverty impoverishing the quality of life for re-
    gions that are reachable,
and in those with the reach who find reason not to reach out
    to treat what is treatable

I see him in disease taking life out of uninfected yet affected families

I see him in oppression, pressing down on the oppressed and the oppressor

I see him in depression, in Prozac and pain pills, in razor blades and bed-side wills

I see him in abuse: physical, mental, emotional misuse

I see him in spiritual confusion, material obsession, physical possessions

I see him in marital transgressions, childhood remorse from an ugly divorce

I see him in our slavery to appearances, appearing to care more about our images than those in dying villages

I see him in our ignorance, ignoring truth for some comfortable inference

I see his emergence in our churches as we pull out emergency verses as deterrents to religious differences, going on the defensive, defending our way of worship, making community worthless

Death is killing us before we even enter the surface of the earth

We are in the service of his words, "It is finished" the end of birth

Oh Death, where is your sting?

Oh Grave, where is your victory?

For we have risen above your misery!
We will not succumb to your finality!
We have overcome your infamous mystery!
In the infinite reign of Christ's ministry!
For we are the resurrection
The insurrection of fatality!
We are the risen deity, the intersection of a dead yet living
body!
We live through imperfections, for we died to become holy!
We cannot be contained by the mouth of the grave
We are the willing slaves to the one who rose from the
garden cave
We have passed through death to new birth
We gave the grave to the earth
And we claim today the cross' worth
The body of his rising
We are the risen church.

—DAVID BOWDEN [1]

SUFFERING WELL

If the church does not recapture its prophetic zeal, it will become an irrelevant social club without moral or spiritual authority. If the church does not participate actively in the struggle for peace and for economic and racial justice, it will forfeit the loyalty of millions and cause men everywhere to say that it has atrophied its will. But if the church will free itself from the shackles of a deadening status quo and, recovering its great historic mission, will speak and act fearlessly and insistently in terms of justice and peace, it will enkindle the imagination of mankind and fire the souls of men, imbuing them with a glowing and ardent love for truth, justice, and peace.

—DR. MARTIN LUTHER KING [1]

God defines us as co-laborers and partners in his kingdom knowing full well that it's not an easy road, that it means we will suffer. Since it is inevitable, we must decide that we are going to suffer well even before it comes. This may seem like a daunting task, but it can be done. It must be done. We must establish disciplines, principles, and a close network of friends committed to this cause. But how? Is it possible to prepare people to suffer with dignity and integrity? How do you teach the discipline of *suffering well* ahead of time?

Take a lesson from the Amish. The Amish raise their children to believe in the power of forgiveness. Even before forgiveness is needed, their children understand that life cannot continue without the extension of forgiveness and reconciliation. So, when a milk truck driver drove into an Amish neighborhood and opened fire in a schoolhouse, killing five children, forgiveness quickly became the big story, even more so than the headline of five murdered children. News reporters were shoving microphones into the faces of parents and grandparents, asking, "How can you forgive in this moment?" Their response was simple: "Because Jesus commands us to forgive." You see, the Lord's Prayer is prayed in every Amish worship service, and when Jesus teaches his disciples how to pray in Matthew 6:14–15, he comes back to one principle—forgiveness.

"For if you forgive others when they sin against you, your heavenly Father will also forgive you. But if you do not forgive others their sins, your Father will not forgive your sins."[2]

The Amish believe that the unwillingness to forgive ultimately puts your salvation in jeopardy. Therefore, they teach their children this principle very early on. The same can be applied in how we prepare our future generations to suffer well.

Kayci and I want to teach our children how to suffer well—even though they are still quite young—because suffering will inevitably come. Sometimes it hurts like a paper cut, and other times it'll be like a slug to the chest. Suffering comes with impact, and it leaves behind images and reminders of its damage. But to allow personal suffering to negatively alter your attitude and behavior can soon turn you into someone you never wanted to become.

In his book *Pilgrim Heart*, Darryl Tippens devotes an entire chapter to the spiritual discipline of suffering. He calls it "the fire that purifies." As a faculty member at Pepperdine University in Malibu, California, Darryl is well aware of the necessity for disaster preparedness. Because of their location, university staff must be prepared for earthquakes, mud slides, brushfires, and even tsunamis. There's a lot of money that goes into preparing the university for disaster, but it's worth it because it prepares them for difficult times.

Most people today don't want to think of suffering as a spiritual discipline. Historically, though, we find examples that teach otherwise. There were once desert fathers—men devoted to intentionally setting aside time for solitude with God in order to pray, fast, and meditate—who would purposefully harm their bodies as a discipline to connect them to the suffering of Jesus. That's taking it a bit too far. But Darryl's onto something profound. The church is at its best when it teaches people to engage the world in a way that says, "We don't care what form of suffering has invaded your life. We are here to walk with you, because that's what Jesus would do."

There is a scene in the movie *We Were Soldiers* that so captured me that I bought the movie just for this one part: while the men are out fighting a battle, the wives are back at the base. One day, a taxi driver pulls up to Lieutenant Colonel Hal Moore's (Mel Gibson's character's) house. His wife, Julie Moore (played by Madeleine Stowe), is home alone, and the moment she sees the taxi she knows this can only mean bad news. (If a taxi driver pulled up to your house at the base, it almost always meant that you were about to be handed a slip of paper announcing that your husband was dead.) She opens the door, and the man says, "Ma'am, I hate to bother you, but do you know where this address is?" She is furious, as any woman would be in that moment.

He begins walking to his car, but before he gets there, he turns around and tells her how much he hates this part of his job. She responds by telling him to bring her every telegram from then on. She wants them in her hands so she can deliver them herself, in person. And she does. Day after day, more telegrams show up on her doorstep, and she hand delivers them. After every telegram is delivered, it is followed by hugs and tears. It is her way of entering into the pain of other people.

We aren't meant to grieve alone. It's part of what it means to discover how to *suffer well.* As uncomfortable, unfriendly, and unwarranted as suffering can be, pain connects us with others. It forms alliances and gives us common ground to connect with people we might never otherwise come into contact with. Few people do community better than pain-ridden people.

The church is made up of hurting, broken, and scarred people. Some of the buzzwords in church circles over the past decade have been "authenticity" and "honesty." You hear more and more pastors urging people to stop being fake and phony, and for good reason. Facades of perfection actually shed a negative light on Jesus. A church with only fixed people isn't the church Jesus died for. Jesus stepped into the suffering of the world rather than hanging back on the edges with the more socially acceptable. He soon found out that living with such passion eventually weeds out your community of friends. Stepping into brokenness often gets you persecuted by the elite; in fact, it might get you killed. But it's a guaranteed place to find God on the move, and it is where we catch glimpses of God's creative and redemptive work.

Paul describes the church as "the ministry of reconciliation."[3] This means that the church must wake up to embrace its calling, to stop running away from our hurting neighbors, but to breathe and speak life into the world we live in. The church isn't the church until it intentionally cultivates time, energy, and resources to engage the world's suffering.

My friend Josh Graves tells a story about a lunch he had with a survivor of the Rwandan genocide in 1994. During that time, almost one million people were slaughtered in three months. It's one of the worst humanitarian crises of the twentieth century—and the U.S. did nothing. Former president Bill Clinton calls it one of the greatest regrets of his life. Josh asked his friend about his experience. He told stories of pain, worry, danger, escape, and provision to come to America. He talked about prophecy, vision, and hope. And then Josh asked him what he does now for a living.

"I'm a pastor," he said. "Now I give my entire life to immigrants in Nashville, helping them to transition linguistically, educationally, professionally, and relationally. I look out for them, the same way others looked out for me. Once you've suffered . . . once you've been swallowed up in pain, you can't help but want to see the pain and suffering of others alleviated. And when you see the pain and suffering of others lifted—you feel alive in a way that is more real than weed, speed, cocaine, alcohol, gambling, and even sex."

That is God's dream for us in this world. It always has been.

A lot of preaching begins with Genesis 3 and the fall, but our Bible begins with Genesis 1 and 2. It's a story of a God who, in the very beginning, *created*. The reason so many voices and writers in Scripture point back to the creation story isn't so much to recount an event in history as to point out that the same God can create something new—*again.*

In a way, Eve becomes a prophet in Genesis 4:1. After being expelled from the garden because of rebellion, Eve gives birth and announces to the world that she was able to produce a child "through the help of the Lord." As the story of Scripture unfolds outside the garden, it begins with a declaration that the partnership God planned with humans would press on. Even though humans were expelled from the garden, punished for their sin, they weren't forgotten. They weren't neglected. The Creator God was going to move, exist, and connect with humans even outside of Eden. God creates and re-creates. This is good news for suffering people.

The rhythm of creation, rebellion, consequence, and God's steadfast commitment to redeem humanity continues to unfold. God hasn't drifted from his initial desire for unity and harmony with his creation. He remains attached to his redeeming story. Through the resurrection of Jesus, he set in motion a furthering of this story, a new initiative: God anointed people. He saw them (and still sees us) as his life-breathing agents. Jesus commissioned broken people to tend to broken people. He wanted them to learn how to take the brokenness of their lives—and the lives of others—and see what God can do.

Two miracles happen in Acts 9 and 10 that reshaped the social makeup of Jesus followers and forced them to surrender their old ways of seeing.

One happens in Acts 9 when Saul encounters the presence of Jesus and is blind for three days until God changes the way Saul sees the world. Saul's name is eventually changed to Paul, which means "small" or "humble." How's that for a new name? But it was so fitting for his mission in the world. Saul was entitled, prideful, narrow-minded, and blind to the greater purposes of God, but not Paul. Paul, despite the meaning of his new name, was a part of God's bigger plan to redeem the earth. The name change brought a new identity and a new vision for the world, one that included people that Saul would never have embraced on his own.

In Acts 10, another conversion takes place. We often label Acts 10 the story about the conversion of Cornelius, but it's just as much about the conversion of Peter. It's not Peter's conversion to Jesus, but it's his conversion to the greater mission of Jesus.

God gives renewed vision to his people in Acts 9 and 10. God is able to energize his people with new eyes for a greater mission. They soon embrace the pain of breaking down social and ethnic barriers, and the world is never the same again.

One of the greatest testaments of God's desire to make all things new is that Jews and Gentiles, rich and poor, the wounded and the scarred, became part of the same family.

This kind of stuff can only happen through the activity and intervention of God. And he's not done yet.

To suffer well, as in the cases of Paul and Peter, is to reset how we think about a world that God is slowly bringing into our current reality. It becomes something we embrace and live. The challenge is that we tend to stick with what we think is possible and then work only within those parameters. We accept certainty because we may not be able to afford to dabble in uncertainties. But God's way is a different way. It's a way of reimagining a world that comes into contact with the resurrection of Jesus. It's a world in need of the news that love defeats hate, reconciliation trumps division, and Jesus is present in every scar.

Nelson Mandela once said, "It always seems impossible until it's done." This is where God wants us to know that we are more than soccer moms, physicians, high school dropouts, prom queens, and retirees. We are people who have been created in God's own image, and God desires partnership. God doesn't just want us to believe in him; he wants us to know that he believes in us.

MercyMe has been on the scene in Christian music for over a decade. Their name originated back when their lead singer, Bart, was a youth minister in Florida. His grandmother was concerned that her grandson was always home whenever she called, so one day she said, "Well *mercy me*, why don't you get a real job?" For some reason, the name stuck.

Bart's dad died when he was eighteen years old. Out of his grief, he began writing a song called "I Can Only Imagine." The song was completed in 1999, but it wasn't released until 2001.

In 2002, it won three separate Dove Awards: Pop Song of the Year, Song of the Year, and Songwriter of the Year. It also soared to number one on the Christian charts, where it remained for years—not days, weeks, or months—but years! Not only did it rule Christian radio, it gained significant airplay on secular radio stations. On 100.3 in Dallas (KJKK), a station known for "Playing What We Want," where you'll hear everything from U2 to Van Halen to Guns N' Roses, callers began requesting "I Can Only Imagine," and the producer began urging for it to be played.

It peaked on the Billboard Hot 100 and Country Songs charts. Over one million copies of the single have been purchased online, which makes it the only Christian song to receive such status. Today on iTunes, it's still listed in the Top 10 Christian songs, and it's been over a decade. My niece was nine when Jenny died, yet the song she chose to play in the background of a mommy/daughter slide show was this one. She wasn't even one year of age when the song was released.

I find it interesting that the song came out in 2001,

right around 9/11, during a time when the United States stood still. For some reason, followers of Jesus and even others who don't claim to follow Jesus found something of hope in this song. It blows my mind that people were craving this song who didn't even believe in heaven or hell.

Could it be that many connected with this song because it offers the hope of dancing with Jesus when all things are fulfilled? Could it be because people wanted to find something better than what we experience day in and day out? There is this itch in the human heart that aches for a world where love has legs. Where hate has been permanently crippled. Where buildings don't crumble and guns don't kill.

God ignites these dreams for a reason, dreams in line with his heart. Instead of looking for his approval of our personal—and sometimes selfish—dreams, maybe we are meant to live in such a way that God's dreams and vision for the world invade our allegiances, priorities, finances, resources, and long-term strategic plans. It is God who restores. And it is God who invites us to be restorers. Be who God has called you to be.

IN THIS TOGETHER

"The future of the church depends on whether it develops
true community. We can get by for a while on size, skilled
communication, and programs to meet every need, but unless
we sense that we belong to each other, with masks off, the
vibrant church of today will become the powerless church
of tomorrow. Stale, irrelevant, a place of pretense where
sufferers suffer alone, where pressure generates conformity
rather than the Spirit creating life—that's where the church is
headed unless it focuses on community."

—LARRY CRABB[1]

Have you ever wondered why God birthed the church
through Pentecost in Acts 2? The idea of community
was already a prominent idea weaving its way throughout Scripture, but in Acts 2 the church is unleashed to be
something special, unique, powerful.

Pentecost wasn't just about conversions; it was about
how the Spirit of God commissioned converted people.

The question wasn't "How do we baptize people?" It went beyond that to ask "How are baptized people supposed to live?" That became a powerful witness to the resurrection of Jesus. Evangelism wasn't just about good preaching; it was about good communal living.

It amazes me how diverse the church became. In fact, the New Testament would be much shorter if Paul had written cities with this message: "Why don't the Jewish Christians meet on the east side of town and the Gentile Christians meet on the west side of town? Schedule an annual night of fellowship once a year, and learn to shake hands in the marketplace." But Paul believed that Jesus had come to establish a new community made up of the prestigious CEOs and the high school dropouts . . . the hospital janitor and the town attorney . . . the white and the black. I would go so far as to say that it was Paul's passion for a unified church that ultimately got him killed.

For some reason, God believes in the church—I'm not talking about the building but the people. You may not like what the church has become. You might feel like it is too institutional. You might feel like you could preach better, lead better, and that if you were in charge things would run more smoothly. You might be connected to a church but withhold your tithe because you are not sure what you're investing in. I'd encourage you to honor the discipline of generosity and become part of reimagining the church as a mission—an outpost—not just a building. Here's what you can't deny—that God loves the church. After all, it was God's idea. God functions and exists within community.

We often talk about the world in Genesis 1 and 2 as being completely perfect. There was harmony, rhythm, and unity in the garden. The word *good* is used each day after God creates ("God saw all that he had made, and it was very good" (Gen. 1:31)). There's a rhythm to the creation story—God speaks, something happens, then God pronounces it as good. It's all good, until Genesis 2:18. Something happens. The cadence of creation changes. Out of nowhere we are blindsided with this statement from God: "It is not good . . ."

Whatever comes after those four words is going to change the story of Scripture. It's going to change how God engages the world. God states, "It is not good for the man to be alone. I will make a helper suitable for him." What does this say about God? Why wouldn't God be the helper? Is God not enough?

John Ortberg writes, "Sometimes in church circles when people feel lonely, we will tell them not to expect too much from human relationships, that there is inside every human being a God-shaped void that no other person can fill. That is true. But apparently, according to the writer of Genesis, God creates inside this man a kind of 'human-shaped void' that God Himself will not fill."[2]

Community, friendships, and relationships—according

to the story of Scripture—aren't an option for people who choose to live in Christ; it is God's way. It is God's intent. It is God's plan.

Have you ever thought about what makes a community a community? It's got to be more than the proximity of two or more human beings, right? You can be in the same room with people without knowing names or one another's stories. It's got to be more than social clubs and sporting events. At some point, for true community to exist, layers have to be pulled off, the surface has to be penetrated, and authenticity must be revealed as the true gift that brings life.

A storytelling community can't ignore the scars and wounds that have shaped us. It's who we are. We can't hide the grief under the rug. We can't scrape the baggage from our identity. We can't remove the unanswered questions we've carried for years. So, God, in his infinite wisdom, created community, because stories are meant to bear witness to something. They are meant to link us to all of humanity.

In 2003, before I even knew about Sycamore View Church, members made the decision to remain in their current location instead of moving farther outside the Memphis city limits. It was something they had wrestled with for a while. After a lengthy season of prayer and fasting, they decided to stay at 1910 Sycamore View Road.

When I interviewed at the church in February of 2008, I saw pictures from a Sunday morning in 2006 when families from the church took crosses out onto the front lawn and nailed them into the ground, forming one large cross. This was a statement that the Sycamore View family was putting their stake in the ground. They were claiming this community as their home, mission field, and neighborhood. I saw these pictures, and I remember thinking, *I could be a part of a story like this. I could join in the mission of a church that has chosen to stay in the fight.*

There was one problem: people actually began praying dangerous prayers, asking that the church begin to reflect the community culturally, ethnically, and economically. I call these prayers dangerous because they were prayers that would get us involved in the business of God. They were prayers through which, if God answered them, racism, entitlement, white privilege, and all forms of pride would be greatly challenged. And God began to move.

Someone once asked, "If your church building burned down, would the surrounding community weep?" It's a question that has taken up residence in the back of my mind.

Through relationships developed between Sycamore View Church and some of the kids in our community, we conducted research and discovered that there were more than one thousand kids in the 38134 zip code who did not have a place to go after school. This is how gang participation increases and how teenage pregnancy runs rampant. Our youth minister, Jim Hinkle, a guy whose heart burns for the city, dove into some deep conversations with the Boys & Girls Clubs of Greater Memphis. While there is a very successful day care next to our church, there was still a great need for a safe place for kids to hang out after school. In June of 2008 we completed the addition of a two-story building on the back of our main structure, which we had been praying for God to use significantly for his kingdom. Jim's conversations led to negotiations, and before we knew it, a branch of the Boys & Girls Clubs of Greater Memphis was operating in our facility.

The transition wasn't completely seamless. We had some people who were worried about our new facility deteriorating, about things being broken or stolen, and all the other things that could happen by having one hundred and fifty kids on our campus at the same time. What if a kid broke an arm? What if we got sued?

Isn't it just reality that kids are going to break arms? If kids are going to break their arms either in gang fights after school or at a church building where people care about their well-being, let them break their arms on our campus. If we get sued, we'll trust God to sort it out.

I'm more concerned about God asking church leaders why there aren't more broken items and scratches on walls—buildings that bear witness to the fact that they have been used—than I am of having a building that is spotless without any blemishes. May God forgive us for taking better care of our buildings than we do our neighbors. May God have mercy on us when capital campaigns aren't asking how our facilities can become hubs for our neighborhoods.

Having the Boys & Girls Club on our campus has presented challenges, but it has also taught us about the thrill of taking risks and joining in the prayer Jesus taught of the kingdom coming *here on earth* as it is in heaven.

Not loving our neighborhoods and cities can't be an option if we are followers of Jesus. Not if we are caught up in the movement. We don't need to choose where our mission field is going to be. We simply need to stand on the front porches of our homes and church buildings and claim what we see before us as precisely where we are called to engage people in deeper ways.

There's a moment in Luke's story of Jesus that grabbed my imagination shortly after I moved to Memphis. I don't know how many times I'd read the story of the triumphal entry before, but this time I noticed that Luke inserts an image that the other Gospel writers ignore.

Luke 19:41: "As he came near and saw the city, he wept over it."

Jesus weeps.

He weeps over Jerusalem.

He weeps over Jerusalem knowing he's about to die in the city.

He weeps over Jerusalem knowing he's about to die in the city so that people can find life.

This verse wouldn't let me go. Jesus isn't driven by pity, but it's a kind of weeping that drives him to action. His tears begged me to ask myself a question that I believe we need to consider individually and corporately:

How are we, the church, joining Jesus in weeping over our contexts with the willingness to lay down our lives, resources, and budgets so that people can find life? Because we aren't called to simply live together but to live together with a purpose.

Entering into the sufferings of the world is the path into God's heart and into the mission of Jesus. The resurrection of Jesus launches the church, the people of God, into his desire to re-create a world that is broken.

Our churches can't afford to be paralyzed by fear. This is too often the case. What if we fail? What if we don't make it? What if it the dream doesn't work? What if we run out of our money?

I heard someone say recently, "I'd rather make a great comeback from failure than to have never attempted something and be average."

I remember something Randy Frazee referred to in

The Connecting Church. He mentioned that geese can go 70 percent farther each day by flying together as a group than if they were to embark on their own journey. Seventy percent!

So, let's go somewhere together. Let's be more fearful of never joining in the adventure. Jesus' invitation isn't just to heaven; it's into the adventure that has already begun.

ALL IN

When our imaginations are stirred we believe in a different kind of world.

A world altered because God makes sense of the mess.

A world that rewards risk.

A world over-flowing with God's justice and mercy.

A world soaked in reconciliation.

A world full of people dancing with God.

Until this world is fully manifested, may those who follow the teachings of the Rabbi from Nazareth conduct and share Jesus Feasts all around the world, in every imaginable space. . . .

—JOSHUA GRAVES[1]

When the church is captured by the thrill of adventure, we strategically permeate the world with the hope of restoration and renewal. The good news that Jesus can reframe the scars of life is compelling, inviting, and contagious. It's because of this hope that I've taken a plunge into this journey. Through suffering, wounds, and scars,

I'm drawn into the daily invitation to follow Jesus with reckless abandonment.

Faith is about a plunge.

I learned the thrill of plunging on my last day of swimming lessons as a kid. No one enrolls their children in swimming lessons with the expectation that their child will only be able to tread water. It's more than that. It's about holding your breath, using your hands and feet, and grabbing coins from the bottom of the pool. Most of all, it's about taking a plunge off the diving board.

I can remember that as I worked my way through the lessons, I glanced up at the high dive and thought to myself that it wasn't that high. That is, until the last day of training when we had to jump off the board. All of a sudden, it had stretched itself to new heights. What once looked like something I could touch with my hand while standing on my tippy-toes was now the height of a three-story building. The grand finale of my lessons was to jump off this thing, and I was cool with it—until I actually stood on it.

I remember walking to the edge wearing nothing but my Superman Speedo. It was just me and the water. And I froze. There was no way I was going to do this. It was a death sentence. I knew that I would eat lima beans or clean my room for three weeks straight instead of taking this plunge. I had turned around to walk off the diving board when my instructor and friends began cheering for me.

They were clapping for me and encouraging me. My mom was over to the side, saying, "Josh, you got this, honey. You can do this." It wasn't a risk like the Wright brothers flying the first plane or Jackie Robinson taking his first swing in the big leagues, but it was a huge risk for me. So, not knowing if I would live to tell about it, I did it. I jumped. I took the plunge.

It was later in life that I learned what it meant to embrace faith as a plunge. Up until that point, Jesus was my mascot. I admired him; I just didn't care to follow him. I was what Dallas Willard calls a vampire Christian— I wanted Jesus for his blood. I knew if I died I'd gladly choose heaven over hell, but it's because there weren't any other options. I had confessed Jesus as Lord, I had been baptized, I was at church every Sunday; I just didn't care about being *all in.* I didn't care to follow Jesus in a way that altered my life. I cared more about Jesus following me to clean up any messes I made and to push me into heaven in case I died.

That is, until God captured my heart by displaying the power of forgiveness in my life. I had gone through a short season of intentional sin. My ego had led me into some destructive life choices. Jenny came home from college that summer and began asking me pointed questions about some of my decisions. She sensed that there were pieces in my life that weren't adding up. Because of our deep relationship, we shared some of our downfalls with each other. Then, she had this idea that we should sit Mom and Dad down and confess our sins. I thought she was off her rocker. What sixteen-year-old wants to confess sins to his parents? But we did it. In tears I shared with my parents some choices I had been making. I didn't expect what happened next. My mom took off running out of the room. I thought she had left the room because of disappointment, but a few moments later, she returned with her Bible opened to Psalms, and she proceeded to pray psalms of forgiveness over her children.

I remember having this Luke 5 moment. In that passage there had been a miraculous catch of fish. Simon Peter threw himself at the feet of Jesus and said, "Go away from me, Lord; I am a sinful man!"

Jesus responded, "Don't be afraid"—the number one command in all of Scripture—"From now on, you will . . ." (NRSV).

This is where Matthew and Mark fill in the blank with *"fishers of men."* But Luke interprets this moment differently. Luke says, "From now on, you will be *catching people."* It's the Greek word *zogreo,* which literally means "to capture alive." So, I had this moment where I thought, *Am I living as someone who has been captured alive for a greater purpose?* I decided then to begin living with the answer, "Yes." I discovered the grace that God extends to sustain people on the journey called life. Jesus invaded my heart, and I was given a new reason to live.

■   ■   ■

The greatest story of deliverance in the Old Testament is when God delivered the Israelites from Egyptian oppression in the book of Exodus. The deliverance story culminates in Exodus 14 when God parts the sea so his people can walk across dry ground.

Here's what I love about Exodus 14: we discover that God doesn't partially deliver people. God doesn't halfway save people. God's intent is total restoration—for all things! God himself is *all in*!

The people were saved walking through water. There was no other way around the sea. They had to go straight through it. In the New Testament, people were saved through water as well. The early church practiced baptism by immersion. You didn't go in ankle deep, knee deep, waste deep, or neck deep; you went all in. It was a plunge.

I'll never forget baptizing a guy in our church named Deairio. He's a tall, stocky fellow. Before I baptized him, he looked down at me and asked, "We're going all the way under, right?"

"Yes, sir," I replied.

He asked a good follow-up question: "Are you going to be able to lift me back up?"

Without a blink I said, "Don't worry, bro, I have about a 76 percent success rate." We laughed, and I got him back up.

God's invitation is to be all in.

What's strange in Exodus is that by chapter 16, the people are ready to go back to Egypt. Strange, huh? They had been oppressed slaves for over four centuries. They tasted freedom. They were led to safe land. And now they wanted to go back.

Could it be that their past was more appealing than a delivered future because it was familiar? Even though the new land would be better, it provided a bad case of the fear of the unknown.

Today, at 201 Poplar in Memphis—the famous city jail that is sung about in rap songs—live a few thousand felons, and 60 percent of them are experiencing at least their sixth sentencing in the jail. Why would men and women who have been released from the confines of prison bars go back into a community and commit further acts that send them right back to the jailhouse? Why not choose freedom? Maybe because the old way is just familiar.

This year, nearly one million heart bypass surgeries will be performed in America. After each one, doctors will advise their patients to change their diets, tend to their bodies, and exercise for good health. However, only 10 percent will take the recommendation. Most will go right back to the lifestyle that warped their bodies in the first place.

And how many times have you seen women who have been abused make a decision to leave their abuser only to end up in another relationship where abuse continues?

God is forging another way. It's a life that is reframed with purpose, meaning, and existence. Just as the scars remained on Jesus after the Resurrection, scars remained on the Israelites after their time in Egypt. The words that defined their experiences in Egypt remained in their vocabulary. God didn't remove the scars as he ushered them into a new land. In fact, he commanded that they retell the story of Egypt to their children, because it was a story that needed to be retold. It was their story. These scars weren't to be ignored; they were meant to be reframed in light of restoration. The scars of life are meant to remind us that we do not have to go back to destruction and oppression. There's a new way.

As God's people left Egypt, they were told that they would plunder the Egyptians. This meant that the households in Egypt would fear the movement of God so much that they'd hand over gold, silver, food, and merchandise. But here's a good question: How much stuff could you carry in the pre–U-Haul era? You didn't have trailers and flatbeds. You had wagons, but how dependable were they? They were limited on what they could take. They had to choose essentials.

Here's what often goes unnoticed. The first possession mentioned once the Israelites reached the other side of the Red Sea was a timbrel, or tambourine. A tambourine!

Read Exodus 15:20 and you'll see it. Of all the essentials they had to carry with them to survive the journey, they made sure to take tambourines.

A tambourine is an instrument for celebration. It wasn't created for lament songs. It was created for celebration and dancing. The women of God took instruments of celebration, and they didn't even know what kind of lyrics were going to fit the story they would be singing. They were simply walking in faith that God was going to do something worth celebrating.

God is concerned about celebration in Scripture. In fact, God commands his people to hold festivals. Some of the festivals were more solemn, because God knows there's a need for confession and meditation. But other festivals were parties. God instructed his people to have massive parties. He wanted them to celebrate with such passion that outsiders would begin to ask, "What is going on in your life worth celebrating with that much time and energy?" And the response is simple: "The Lord has done great things for us, and we are filled with joy" (Psalm 126:3).

Jesus attended parties. He threw them. In fact, he even encouraged his followers to throw parties for people who would never invite them back. Jesus knew that life with him was worth celebrating. In the story of the prodigal son in Luke 15, when the younger son returns from going wild, there was a party thrown in which you could hear "music and dancing." It's one thing to hear music; it's another thing when you can hear dancing.

This is the appropriate response when the stories of redeemed scars are told.

A scar is a healed wound. The danger in life is when we don't allow wounds to become scars. We continue to pick, irritate, and poke at scabs, and this isn't good for our health. Only when we acknowledge the wounds in our hearts will scars begin to be redeemed.

Danielle Hacker came to Sycamore View as a scarred woman. Low self-esteem led her into deep depression. Her attempt to self-medicate came through hard-core drugs, alcohol, and sex. They were things she knew were wrong, but they provided small moments of relief from the greater emotional pain going on inside.

She reached a low point in January of 2012, when not even cocaine or liquor could mask the hurt. The pain was so deep that she decided to end her life. She took forty-three Geodon and, a few hours later, found herself in the emergency room. Unable to explain how she was still alive, the doctors treated her in the ICU for three days before releasing her to Lakeside Behavioral Health System in Memphis.

After a couple of phone conversations and numerous visits from friends, Danielle engaged me in a deeper conversation about Jesus. She decided that she wanted to be baptized and that she wanted her testimony shared before her baptism.

I stood in the water looking out over Sycamore View Church with Danielle, and I had her lift her arms in the air. Danielle had been a cutter. When narcotics and stimulants didn't provide the fix she desired, she resorted to cutting. She had scars all the way from her wrists to her elbows. I told her and the church that the scars would be there for life. The salvation of God doesn't remove them. But the power of God can free her from the emotional and psychological baggage of her past. After her baptism, there was celebration.

We hold these stories as sacred; we celebrate how they have been redeemed. Let the followers of Jesus reclaim the need to live with anticipation that God is doing things worth celebrating, and when God redeems, let's throw some of the best parties this world has ever known. The clock is ticking on injustice, and there is a day on its way when God will make all things right. Yet, in Jesus, we are reminded that God's way is in this day. He is healing the world. Through scars and all, let's be all in!

ACKNOWLEDGMENTS

There are countless stories of others who have chosen to suffer well. I have heard many of them firsthand. I've also seen them depicted in movies, books, and in blogs. These stories always strike a chord with me, and they have shaped and formed my heart and the content of this book.

Thanks to 5-hour ENERGY for shocking my body throughout this entire writing process. You performed well to keep me up at night when I needed to stay awake, and you gave me the necessary boost in the morning after 3:00 a.m. writing sessions. I'm close to being in rehab now to treat my energy drink addiction, but thank you for helping me along the way.

On a serious note, several friends read through early rough drafts of this book. It was when I felt like I had a story to tell, but I wasn't sure how it would all fit together. These friends wrestled with me and gave me the constructive criticism needed to make this into the book it is now. Thank you, Mike Cope, Chris Seidman, Rick Atchley, Jerry

Taylor, Luke Norsworthy, Kristi Hartman, Collin Packer, Troy Robertson, Jonathan Storment, Pam Cope, and Lynn Anderson.

A special thanks to Sara Barton, whose attention to detail pushed me in areas I didn't know I needed to be pushed. And to my boy, Josh Graves, who constantly encouraged me to find my writing voice. You've been a true companion and a trusted friend as this book unfolded.

To my agent, Wes Yoder, I'm still stunned that a man of your caliber chose to take on a first-time author like myself, but thanks for believing in me and the story of this book.

To the Howard Books/Simon & Schuster team, thank you for believing in this project and for helping me find my writing voice. As a pastor, I've spent more than ten years writing for the ear in order to be heard. Writing for the eye has been a challenge. Yet, you have inspired, encouraged, critiqued, and affirmed me to believe in the power of words as they come to life. To my editor, Jessica Wong, it has been a joy to work with you. Your attention to detail and ability to find the right word to bring an entire paragraph to life is remarkable. It has been an honor to partner with you on this journey.

I wouldn't be who I am without the congregations I've served who have taught me what it means to suffer well and to suffer with the world. Thank you, Highland Oaks Church in Dallas, Highland Church in Abilene, the Avenue B Church in Ballinger, and to the Southwest Central Church in Houston.

Much of the content in this book wouldn't exist if the Sycamore View church hadn't given a young twenty-seven-year-old an opportunity to join them in 2008. Preaching for you every Sunday, living life with you, and suffering with you as a church that's on a mission has given me so much energy and passion to live life with more purpose. You point me to Jesus.

Though we've never met and we've only exchanged a few emails, I wouldn't be where I am with God if it weren't for Philip Yancey. Of the top ten books I've read in my life, five of them are by Yancey. He has taught me that in life it is okay to ask hard questions, even if we aren't given concrete answers.

I was only sixteen years old, but I'll never forget the day Steve Bragg, my offensive coordinator at Mesquite's Poteet High School, left practice when he received the news that his wife had taken a turn for the worst. She died that evening from kidney failure. After her traffic death, Coach Bragg continued to engage dozens of teenagers as a coach but, more important, as a mentor and a man of integrity. Coach Bragg, even in our thirties, we give you thanks for believing in us. You taught me how to live with integrity, no matter the circumstances.

Every member of my family has played a vital role in altering my life to pursue the Jesus Way with passion. Cecil and Barbie, what maturity I have wouldn't have happened without you.

Dad and Mom, you nurtured me and gave me permission to dream kingdom-size dreams. You are two of my heroes.

Jonathan, you are everything a brother should be. I'm glad we got over our competiveness and sibling rivalries in order to become good friends.

David and Malaya, Jenny gave us you, and you are vital pieces of our family. David, the temporary sting of death continues, but we press on together. Malaya, we will continue to fight for your faith. You are a treasure to us.

Truitt and Noah, I can't wait to come home from work every day to be with you. Kayci and I want to raise you to both escape and engage the suffering of the world. Our prayer is for you to have a gospel imagination.

And last but not least, Kayci Joy, you inspire me like none other. Being married to you is the greatest gift in my life. We have celebrated ten wonderful years together. Yet, I believe that the best years of our marriage are still to come. Let's grow old together.

SCARRED FAITH

JOSH ROSS

Introduction

God is present at all times. This does not mean that he will shield you from life's painful experiences, but he will be with you through it all. The story of scripture depicts a scar-filled world, but it also hangs its existence on the hope that God is at work to repair our brokenness. It is up to us not just to observe it, but to participate in the greater story of restoration. It is this partnership that makes our doubts and pain allies of deep faith, as we open our hearts to allow God's redeeming work in spite of and through the questions.

Topics and Questions for Discussion

1. When Jenny's health was deteriorating Josh's mom urged those who had gathered in the hospital not to get upset and, "serve any other gods." (p. 30) Have you ever been tempted to serve another god during a challenging time? If so, how did you work through the struggle? If not, what kept you from going down that path?

2. Josh talks about asking God to intervene and save Jenny, but ultimately, she slips away. When have you prayed for something that you feel went unanswered? Did you ever find peace or see that God answered in a different way than expected?

3. On p. 41, Josh asks the question, "What does it mean to be a disciple when we don't get our way?" Have you ever been tempted to "unfollow" Jesus, as some of his disciples did when they realized the journey would be different than they expected? What are some lessons you have learned along the way about surrender?

4. What do you think the Ross family's use of CarePages (pp. 43–45) says about the connection between suffering and community?

5. How do you feel about the song that Josh's family posted

while they were grieving over Jenny's death? Can you relate to the sentiments expressed in the lyrics?

6. Josh comments that "Maybe we force others into celebratory moods when many need to know that God can meet them where they are." (p. 48) What was a time in your life when you needed the God who meets you where you are? How was this healing in its own way?

7. In one of Josh's journal entries after Jenny's death, he bares his anger and frustration with God. Have you ever felt anger like that toward God? Did you allow yourself to share your anger with Him?

8. Why do you think Josh felt he needed God to "cry with him?" (p. 61) How do you think this helped him during this difficult time?

9. Josh describes how his baptism makes him a "participant in the rhythm of creation" (p. 94) and how this no longer allows him to push aside the brokenness he sees around him. What does it mean to be a "participant," and do you see yourself in this way?

10. How would you describe what it means to ra'ah (pp. 104–105)? Have you ever experienced a moment when you felt you've "seen" the world?

11. In Chapter 10, Josh talks about how stepping into the suffering of the world can result in persecution, but it also allows you to see God moving. Have you been hanging back or stepping into the suffering in

your community? How have you seen a glimpse of God's redemptive work?

12. Reflect on your own story. Can you see God's presence in your life when you reflect upon your emotional, spiritual, or physical scars?

Enhance Your Book Club

1. Josh uses the example of the song his friends wrote—"Some Explaining to Do"—to describe how he and his family felt after Jenny's death. (pp. 45–46) The song is sometimes controversial and asks God for answers, but Josh writes that it helped him and his family deal with their suffering. Write and share a poem or song to express how you've felt in the middle of a difficult time.

2. Similar to what Josh had to do in seminary, come up with your own metaphor to describe your faith, and share and discuss with your book club members.

3. As the Rwandan pastor shared, "once you've been swallowed up in pain, you can't help but want to see the pain and suffering of others alleviated." (p. 132) As a group, commit to a number of community service or volunteer hours to accomplish over a year, and plan volunteer activities that can be accomplished together as a group.

NOTES

Introduction: Scarred Faith

1. Philip Yancey, *The Jesus I Never Knew* (Grand Rapids, MI: Zondervan, 1995), 17.

Part 1: When Scars Run Deep

1. Rob Bell, *Drops Like Stars* (Grand Rapids, MI: Zondervan, 2009), 24.

Chapter 1: Does God Make Wrong Turns?

1. Nicholas Wolterstorff, *Lament for a Son* (Grand Rapids, MI: Eerdmans, 1987), 81.
2. Mark 11:9.

Chapter 2: The February from Hell

1. Anne Lamott, *Traveling Mercies* (New York: Anchor Books, 1999), 68.
2. Matthew 7:7–8.
3. Mark 11:24.
4. John 15:7.

Chapter 3: Walking with a Limp

1. Mike Cope, *Megan's Secrets* (Abilene, TX: Leafwood Publishing, 2011), 144–45.
2. KidStand—www.kidstand.org.
3. Dr. Martin Luther King Jr., "I've Been to the Mountaintop" (speech, Mason Temple, Memphis, TN, April 3, 1968).
4. John 6:66.

Chapter 4: Being a Disciple When We Don't Get Our Way

1. Anne Lamott, *Traveling Mercies* (New York: Anchor, 1999), 142.
2. Used by permission of Karen Taylor-Good (www.KarenTaylorGood.com) and Lisa Aschmann (www.lisaaschmann.com).
3. Luke 18:29–30.

Chapter 5: When God Gets Low

1. Nicholas Wolterstorff, *Lament for a Son* (Grand Rapids, MI: Eerdmans 1987), 81.
2. Hebrews 5:7.
3. John 1:14.
4. Exodus 2:23–25.
5. Philippians 2:7.

Part 2: Living with Scars

1. Barbara Brown Taylor, *An Altar in the World* (New York: HarperCollins, 2009), 7.

Chapter 6: Initiated into Undesired Clubs

1. Mother Teresa, *Mother Teresa: Come Be My Light,* edited and with Commentary by Brian Kolodiejchuk, M.C. (New York: Doubleday, 2007), 186–87.
2. Exodus 34:7.

Chapter 7: Is Memphis in Texas?

1. Francis Chan with Danae Yankoski, *Crazy Love* (Colorado Springs, CO: David C. Cook, 2008), 48.

Chapter 8: Lived Experiences

1. Donald Miller, *A Million Miles in a Thousand Years* (Nashville, TN: Thomas Nelson, 2009), 60, 98.
2. Matthew 15:21.
3. Matthew 16:13.
4. Matthew 16:13–20.

Chapter 9: Cursing Toddlers

1. John Irving, *A Prayer for Owen Meany* (New York: Modern Library, 2002), 289.
2. "At-risk neighborhoods" are defined as communities where the social and economic conditions are so poor that moral, emotional, and communal challenges to health are created.
3. "Swing neighborhoods" are defined as communities that could swing in a positive or negative direction in the coming years.
4. Philippians 3:10.
5. Matthew 19:16.
6. Matthew 19:17.

Part 3: Scarred Communities

1. Written and performed by David Bowden. Used by permission. David follows the tradition of the beat poets of the 1950s and slam poets of the 1980s. He uses poetry to challenge and inspire individuals and groups, to give voice to the voiceless, promote social justice, and care for the needy throughout the world. (See http://davidbowdenpoetry.com/about.)

Chapter 10: Suffering Well

1. Dr. Martin Luther King Jr., *A Knock at Midnight*, edited by Peter Holloran and Clayborne Carson (New York: Warner Books, 2000), 73.
2. Matthew 6:14–15.
3. 2 Corinthians 5:18.

Chapter 11: In This Together

1. Larry Crabb, Foreword to *The Connecting Church*, by Randy Frazee (Grand Rapids, MI: Zondervan, 2001), 13.
2. John Ortberg, *Everybody's Normal Till You Get to Know Them* (Grand Rapids, MI: Zondervan, 2003), 32.

Chapter 12: All In

1. Josh Graves, *The Feast* (Abilene, TX: Leafwood, 2009), 157.

A portion of the royalties from
Scarred Faith **will be donated to the following**
two non-profit organizations.

The Touch A Life Foundation rescues, rehabilitates, and empowers exploited, at-risk, and trafficked children in Ghana, West Africa. To learn more about how you can get involved with the organization's work, visit www .touchalifekids.org.

Agape Child & Family Services, Inc., is dedicated to serving children and families who are in need of restoration. Agape works with women who are homeless, children who are in need of permanent and loving relationships, and neighborhoods that are actively seeking engagement with community resources. Agape aims to provide services that strengthen the local community and empower those who live within it. For more information, visit www .AgapeMeansLove.org.